war… &after

---

the anthology of poet warriors

---

collection 2

Publisher: Dead Reckoning Collective
Book Cover Art: Sarah Rosetti

First Edition: November 2020
Printed in the United States of America

ISBN-13: 978-1-7338099-2-4 (paperback)

INTRODUCTION

War is a juggernaut of a subject because war is among the most complex of human experiences. War is as robust a topic to tackle as love or death, even for the most seasoned writer. This is in part because no two experiences are the same. As a result, the phenomenon of war has left us with as many perspectives as casualties.

From the perspective of philosopher, academic, and politician, John Stuart Mill, "War is an ugly thing, but not the ugliest of things. The decayed and degraded state of patriotic feeling which thinks that nothing is worth war is far worse."

Conversely, one of the most renowned, intelligent humans in history, Albert Einstein said of war, "It is my conviction that killing under the cloak of war is nothing but an act of murder."

It is my personal belief that this conviction, existing simultaneously in the minds of many of war's participants, alongside the patriotic feeling which hails them a hero, lends heavily to the cognitive dissonance and subsequent psychological turmoil experienced by many veterans of war. Which happens to be covered by many contributors to this book.

While each of these perspectives are no doubt as elegant as they are valuable, neither was gained from hands-on experience with the subject. In fact, a great deal of the opinions, perspectives, stories, and even poetry about what war is and how it impacts its participants come from people with a second-hand perspective.

The purpose of this collection is not necessarily to host exclusively the greatest poets of our generation (although there are a few in here who may be up to the task) but rather to give to the people an unadulterated, unfiltered window into the emotional and psychological realities of those who have volunteered to go to war.

No definitive prompts were given. The only stipulation to be considered for inclusion into this volume was that those submitting have served in the armed forces.

We received a landslide of submissions. More than double the amount of the first volume, *In Love... &War*. Initially, the thought was to divide the entries into the four pre-existing categories from volume 1 (Preludes and Prologues, In Love, &War, Epilogues and Epitaphs) and call it a day. It became evident, however, after reading the submissions that these poems do not fit into the original container. So, we changed the container.

Of all the poems received, there were two clear and evident themes present: war (direct and general experience) and after. Interestingly, the majority of the poems we received dealt more with the veteran's post-war experience. Topics like going to college, dealing with loss of friends, recurring dreams, recovery, and the love that saw them through, were the meat in this meat and potatoes meal.

While this collection does have a loose organizational structure, this volume does not contain clearly defined sections as many of these poems explore several topics simultaneously. Several poems herein are journeys which meld the arcing lines of experience from war through loss and grief, comforted by love which is often tragically polluted by the war still raging internally.

Many of the poems that were submitted essentially said the exact same thing. When that happened, the one with the more crisp, descriptive, and original syntax was selected.

I want to take this opportunity to say thank you to every single person who had the intestinal fortitude to submit their writing. Picking a scab from your heart and putting it to words is difficult. Pushing send knowing that the wound may be shared with the world is an experience of unparalleled vulnerability. It is my opinion that many from our community could benefit from a little more vulnerability. Much respect to you for shouldering that discomfort for the benefit of others.

To the homies at Dead Reckoning Collective, who have made it their mission to shine a light on veterans living well (and who called me the big brother they never wanted), I give you my thanks and respect. You are a beacon for those with a mind for literature and a heart for war.

Thank you Sarah Rossetti (InvaderGirl) who provided the incredible artwork for this book, including the cover, and who has become one of the strongest and most valuable visual artists for our generation of veterans.

Thank you to you, the reader. By purchasing this book, you contributed to a smoother transition for a veteran. By reading this book, you are sharing the burden of responsibility that comes with the experience of war, one which many contributors to this collection have carried alone for far too long.

A great poet with significant first-hand experience with war by the name of Walt Whitman wrote, "The real war will never get in the books."

Challenge accepted, Walt.

-leo jenkins

Shades
Cokie

Our countrymen look with their feigned interest high
upon our long hist'ry of wars, both past and the nigh.
They see a checked board with its black and its white;
"Our" good and "Their" bad to divide in sight.

The tribes and the beasts of our frayed foes' desires
surely contrast with these angels of ours!
But what if yon checkerboard held no white knights,
no ivory pawns, the darkness to fight?

What if our pieces were rather more red
from stomping the guts and the bones of the dead?
What if the pieces which protected you
were closer to darkness than ever you knew?

"I've gone to war, I've missed your laughs."

Said the Poet to the Warrior

Cooper Thompson

write
said the poet to the warrior
write until your brain hurts your fingers hurt
you are no stranger to pain to struggle
write so that your hands know the relief of a full stop
like your lips know how good water can taste
after days, weeks
pack laden
in the searing heat
have you ever worked so furiously
that water has tasted golden?
like syrup, like medicine?
well then good, you must work that hard once more
do not rest, do not take a knee
do not look back
there is nothing for you back there
write
and you will know victory
write
and you will know peace.

The Poet

Hugh McNulty

Word: a single distinct meaningful element of speech or writing.
Pluralised they can be enlightening, from the pens of war poets they can be frightening, stomach churning and chest tightening.
The brutal honesty and fearful truth of Siegfried Sassoon with his "brave brown companions never came home".
They found their Valhalla somewhere in France but they never died alone.
Wilfred Owen and his Futility "wishing we were all at home, whispering of fields unsown". As we visit the headstones each and every one unknown.
And to Robert Graves and A Dead Boche "To you who'd read my songs of war" with horror he delivers the words of blood and gore "Dribbling black blood from nose and beard".
And from my eye a tear is cleared.
"That there's some corner of a foreign field That is forever England".
The reason I write is Rupert Brooke who says it all in The Soldier.
Don't ever forget that foreign field, it's the reason you and I have the chance to grow older.

The Over-Dramatic Private

Cokie

I entered the Corps a young boy,
my flesh plumped with unabated life.
Hardship I thought I'd known at the hands
of drill and combat instructors,
but I'd not yet known the shattering wrath of the Squad Leader.
The screaming giants ruled the millimeters of existence
with the law of the fist,
demanding steel from my clammy, sweaty soul.
They cursed my weakness, those men with a countenance leathered by the
desert-dry blasts of hate.
They cursed my frailty with words like maces,
elaborate verses like swords wrought in combat.
They told me of their grim, black war,
and sang the songs of iron and slaughter.
My timid irises widened in wonder
as I listened, open mouthed with staccato breath
to their tales of killing and dying
in the soils of Iraq perfumed with palms
and shrapnel;
that place where fear flew like ragged pennants
torn in a swift-rising wind.
Our fated departure to war sent beach waves of terror shuddering through
my spine,
my heart was a house fragranced with piss,
the whites of my eyes widened as sheets,
the panicked entreaties of prey amid the hunt.
Yet the ancestry of my animal brain
and the call of my God invited, yes, demanded courage
to evolve and create myself anew.
Forward I had to march on hardening feet,
forward to drive on detonating roads,
forward to ride in creaking turrets,
and forward the sinews of my life lengthened and strengthened
until the fat of ease was boiled from my bones,
and I became like them,
and one of them.

Arma Virumque Canto

Moises Machuca

I place before you a short-lived Marines'
History, read it if you can. The war
Between them, the others, and us, brothers
See how those who walk and drive outside, grunts,
Form a collective from the lonely;
How in friendship we are *inimicus.*

Woe to her who has no *inimicus*
Those constructed and issued to Marines
Ready to bite foreign soil and grunts
In company to exhale the lonely
Thoughts circulating her mind of war
Known to her, *inimicus*, and brothers.

Rarrus avis in animo, brothers:
Pax; from its discourse with *inimicus*
There she finds her sorrow and the lonely
Both weeping and rejoicing for the war.
Like Ulysses and his men, so Marines
Prefer "*arma virumque*" say the grunts.

Ah, you disgruntled white-sock-wearing grunts
Has your tourniquet preserved your brothers'
Memory, or did it bleed out at war?
Here come boots with worn-out souls, the Marines,
Tripping over the dead *inimicus*
Whose memory makes thee cold and lonely.

Verily, as the mountain looms lonely
Standing watch, it invites its kin the grunts
To ascend and lay a cross for Marines
Whose frame and mind keep no *inimicus*
Whose ceasing of breath makes strangers brothers
Who come from the gluttonous womb of war.

Sing high praises for those laid low at war
Sons and daughters who bequeath us lonely
Terms of agreement. O, *inimicus*
Let's meet again and embrace like brothers
At the parade deck where marching and grunts
Of joy ring in the newly formed Marines.

Marines, no matter whether P.O.Gs or grunts
The war has done away with all lonely
Brothers. We have no more *inimicus*

*(Inimicus: Latin <u>enemy</u> (someone who is hostile to, feels hatred towards,
opposes the interests of, or intends injury to someone else)*

The Day Before

James Freeman

it seems ideal, mid afternoon in March
Alabama is kind—the weather is a gracious mistress
cool and clear
no small wonder we sit here
swaying on porch swings meant for better moments
for fathers and sons to joke, laugh, find themselves covered with ice cream melted
maternal scowls down the road disregarded
i don't know how to do this, i'm not sure my father did either it was easier when you were smaller
when you didn't notice my packed bags
the not so subtle shifts
when you didn't know how to feel Impending or Absence you shouldn't—and yet
i gotta go, my boy, and i'll be back when i can—know that i will
your daddy has gypsy blood and a taste for discord—perfect prerequisites for work on the far flung reaches of our national dominion
i may be gone, but you are never far from me
a baby sock in my left breast pocket
your old favorite friend, Mr. Dangly Man, tucked into my ruck pictures of you —little you—hidden in my cap
i was young the first time i left you—i feel younger still i won't let tears fall, not on this swing, not with you
i might be getting better at this
i hate that
you were young the first time i left—ten days of age and yet—you are older now
someday you'll be as childishly old as me
still, i'll always see you as i do now
herculean locks, little long legs, tiny tank tops
my first born son
it isn't fair of me to ask, i know
but listen as hard as you can, attentively
to words i heard when i was your age, not so long ago
little one, i love you
you are the man of the house now
take care of your mother, see you soon
pause, blink, swallow, breathe, breathe it isn't fair of me to ask, i know—i do but
please
please
don't forget me

Before and After

Matt Coffey

2012
I, State-your-Name-here, do solemnly swear,
Dude, I'm finally doing it!
That I will support and defend
This is it. I'm gonna be a warrior.
The Constitution on the United States
Call of Duty, motherfucker.
Against all enemies, foreign and domestic
Gonna stack so many bodies.
That I will bear true faith and allegiance to the same... Gonna get a knife kill.
Watch out, hajis.

2017
Sir, the weather is a high of 104 and hazy
35D... What was I thinking?
So no change over the past six months.
I'm not Audie Murphy,
The Khalid bin Walid Army's been active in social media, I'm just Dilbert in
uniform.
So these towns are off limits
Never thought I'd serve,
For MWR activities.
And still feel guilty for not serving.

Through My Eyes (Look My Child)

Michael Kelvington

Through my eyes, you'll never see
The pain, the loss, the endured suffering.
Look my child, on your behalf
I've gone to war, I've missed your laughs.
Through my eyes, I've fought and bled,
I've survived some blasts, felt frag's hot shreds.
Look my child, I pray you'll never wear
The lead-filled vest of survivor's guilt and despair.
Through my eyes, I've seen children like you
Live in poverty and squalor, and the fear of guns too.
I've seen a mortar barrage turn life to death,
Stared in lifeless eyes, where a street ran red.
And just in kind, I've watched you grow up from afar,
Denied myself the best years with you thus far.
I've left your mom alone, in an empty home,
No warm body next to hers, or hand to hold.
Meanwhile, through my eyes, I've seen men ripped in half,
Serving others they loved, on your behalf.
Look my child, I'll never get back,
The years I've lost in places like Iraq.
I once walked through a field picking up pieces of a friend,
To return him to his family and tribe I tried to defend.
Through my eyes, I've seen a girl held hostage,
Worked with Afghan friends to liberate her from bondage.
Look my child, I've left you and your siblings alone,
To protect our homeland and defend our home.
Through my eyes, that price has come at a cost,
Gold Star Families' lives destroyed from Soldiers I've lost.
It's through these eyes I've often felt torn,
Being so far from you because of the oath I've sworn.
Look my child, I'm proud of my service,
Leading other sons and daughters, seeing their courage in my presence.
But through my eyes I've seen the hole left in my place,
The empty chair at the dinner table, heads bowed saying grace.
Look my child, I hope someday you'll see,
Not the same experiences my eyes received,
But an understanding that will provide me relief,
That I serve with distinction for a cause I believed.
Look my child, I adore your resilience,
You thrive in this life, despite my absence.
Through my eyes, my greatest of fears,
Is for you to reject me, because I'm hardly here.
Look my child, I love you more than you know,
But with wolves at the door, you know daddy must go.
I know because of the brave, we're the land of the free,
Through my eyes, I feel the calling and say, "Here am I, send me."

Now Is The Hour of Combat's Red Fire

Cokie

Now is the hour of combat's red fire
A river of life that is ended in full
Forever we bleed on the altar of fate
Enslaved by the might of war's powerful pull

Facing the wrath of the cavalry's charge
And claiming that victory mentally wrought,
Battl'ng the cowardice drowning our souls
For all that we've done and all that we ought

Faces of living and bravery one,
We stand at the gates of our savagery bold.
Peering through hell and then finding it sane,
The image of strife that is desp'rate and old.

Withstanding the nature of warlike mankind
Is not in our fate to be darkly foreseen.
Rather we throw ourselves into the fray
Locking and loading as death-bound machines.

Christmas in Afghanistan – 2001

John Dailey

A moonless road on a cheerless December
Pins in my toes and long johns two-sizes too big.
The pickup was piled with packages and people
Pulled to a stop by a garland of razor wire wrapping an axle.
The men in the truck bed wore blankets
Over their shoulders and heads against the cold.
Blankets that snagged at the barrels
And stocks of their AKs.
They struggled and stared.
We watched them
Washed in the red glow of a taillight.
Our frozen fingers bent inside
Torn wool gloves to squeeze our triggers.
Bolt to buffer to stock to shoulder
Eyes pressed to the cold rubber eyecups of night vision.
Road, sand, snow, blood
All shades of green.

Clowns in Amman
Aaron Kirk

They are two and they are sad-looking, thrift-store clowns with regifted smiles. They dance in the middle of the First Circle. Dirty taxis drive around them. I am drunk and I am sad-looking as well but the man sitting across from me is British and he has great teeth, which is a surprise. He buttons his plaid shirt all the way up, the way they do in Europe. We sit in plastic chairs while the waiter brings us Efes beer. The twenty year-old study abroad students who find it a thrill to drink in public begin to whisper because the waiter has a small mullet.

None of the students have a good accent when they try to speak Arabic. I watch the clowns.

They dance in the circle and the drivers ignore them but they frolic anyway. Their makeup reminds me of bootleg DVDs you find in *wasat al-balad* shops for a dollar. The British man works for some international organization and the red-haired girl sitting next to me is drunker than she should be and her laugh is ugly. We are downstairs. There are families with Hijab-wearing mothers and Polo-shirt fathers smoking shishah and making faces at us for not being *a'adi* enough.

I watch the second-rate clowns. They are talking to two very serious-looking Arab men who have guns on their hips and who are probably Mukhabarat. The clowns wear orange. They are not *a'adi*.

The woman sitting across from me with Avril Lavigne hair and an iPhone asks me a question about Yale. I stop watching the clowns. I don't go to Yale, I answer. No, she goes to Yale, she explains. I am sorry, I was not listening. I was watching the clowns, I say. What clowns, she asks.

I look at the circle. They are gone. Everything is *a'adi* again.

Dark Matters

Jennifer Sierra

Twinkles in the sky
Lights strewn across a dark horizon
Like multi-colored fireflies
The beauty of her city's skyline was all she knew
Until she saw the darkest dark of desert hues
In a war-torn land she lay upon a cool concrete barrier
Her eyes set on all they gazed
Never suspecting the stars would betray her
But that betrayal is a story best saved for another day
In this moment she is happy
In this moment before day breaks
She finds her peace
And in this moment and only for a moment she forgets...
The pain, the sadness, the emptiness she feels
Never suspecting it would only get worse
Fixing her stare upon the dark glittering sky
Became her solace in this forsaken place
For she reflected on life back home
And the stark simplicity of life on this base
In these moments she is at peace
Never knowing parts of her soul were claimed
As she lay on that concrete barrier
In awe of the stars she had never seen

Goodnight My Love

John "JT" Tysver

I lay here with your picture beside me.
Even in this Hell I find myself smiling as I close my eyes and can almost feel those
Strands of hair on my arm assuring how close you are to my body.
The alarm sounds again.
I tuck you safely into my body armor.
Even though we have been this distant so many times before I cannot bear
The thought of being away from you.
Just know if i fall tonight, my love;
I will grasp this photo of a smiling woman over my heart.
And I will kiss you goodnight before I fall asleep beside you one last time.

Sangin
Neville Johnson

Sangin days
Sangin nights
Some days I remember
Some days I choose to forget
Other days I miss
Oh Sangin town
My wonderful wild

Misfire

Erik Villasenor

Every machine gunners dream
Positive ID
Enemy in the middle of the street
He shot from the the hip
Pray and spray
This is it
Today is the day
Rounds snapped over head
The air filled with the whispers of ricocheted lead
I shouldered the 240
Took aim
Center mass in my scope
This is it
My moment
Or so I hope
Time stood still
Only me and my respiration
My mind is clear and without hesitation
I squeeze the trigger and
Misfire…

Point Man

Ben Fleming

We set out the gate on a night patrol,
Our mission to disrupt the Taliban's AO,
Our Ops box permitted to cross the canal,
We'd cover the ground that our allies could not.
I volunteered in order to lead from the front,
Point man I'd be for our night time hunt,
A game of roulette with no ground sign to see,
Under this next step could my IED be?
The night was silent except for the dogs barking loud,
My time came to lead the patrol across open ground,
If we were going to get it, here's where it would be,
I stepped off just waiting to hear the AK's sing,
As I moved a deafening burst made me hit the deck,
The boss sends "contact wait out" over the net,
Soon the laughter and giggles made their way forward,
It was just the boys ensuring a dog's bite was thwarted,
War is fun sometimes, the humour's just morbid.

Experiences May Vary: a haiku
Chad Baon

Inside of Iraq,
Starbucks replaced by Green Beans.
Alas, war is Hell.

Gruntled Veteran

Spencer Jacobson

I'm happy with my service
Hard to believe it but, I am.
I went cool places and did great things
In many foreign lands.
My service is not yet over,
In fact, it begins anew.
Whether three more years or twenty,
I'll be glad to see it through.
You see I fight my wars with pencils,
From air conditioned huts.
Watching contractors build buildings,
And tighten aircraft nuts.
It is not the same for every vet,
There're many varied miles.
I realize I have had it good,
And in the end, I'll just have smiles.
It's not to say that it's not been hard,
Or that the path has not been coarse.
What it means is that I'm sure glad,
I chose to join the AirForce.

To the NCOs
Spencer Jacobson

As an Ell Tee I owed a lot,
To those crusty NCOs.
They took me under their wings,
And taught me what they know.
Even my Airmen are owed,
So much gratuity.
For working hard and kicking ass,
Despite the new Ell Tee.
For helping me I thank you all,
I hope that I pulled through.
I've added rank, I've done quite well,
And it's largely thanks to you.

Multi Domain Operations

Ben Fortier

The armies that will withstand the future must have
The capability and will
To dominate all facets of war.
While the peril of nuclear holocaust
Created a deep worry in State actors,
They found subversive tactics
That would fool the observers
And solidify their victory.
There is always a way around
The boundaries of legislation.
Instantaneous communication
Leads to belt fed propaganda machines
Spewing memes of divisive content
Controlled by the same State actors
That are claiming no offensive is currently ongoing.
While masked troops with rifles
And wheeled, armored vehicles with machine guns
Roll through the streets of some village.
News reports claim mercenaries while
Intelligence analysts believe their rivals
Are simply warming up the gears
Of their newly formed war machine. Internet operations
Cyber based warfare
Multi-faceted tactical scenarios
Winning battles without ever firing a shot.

To Get to You
Paula Putrino

To get to you my journey begins...
To get to you I raised my right hand.
To get to you I made my mother cry.
I carried your last name to make it a proud name.
I traveled overseas to prove to you I mattered.
To get to you I saw death, bloodshed, and tears.
To get to you I saw those willing to give it all.
To get to you I found strength within myself.
In my journey to
get to you I learned who I was.
To get to you I faced all I could face.
To get to you I grew from that small town girl.
To get to you I traveled to austere places unknown.
To get to you I traveled to these places always alone.
In this journey, I understood your rage,
Your fears, and discovered myself.
To get to you I experienced anger and hope.
To get to you I found pieces of you in others.
To get to you I am the woman I am today.
To get to you I saw death, bloodshed and tears.
To get to you I saw those willing to give it all.
To get to you I found strength within myself.
Dad—
I carried your name on my chest through it all.
I carried the pride you had on our uniform.
I carried the anger, the burden and the honor too.
All to get to you.

Choices

Jacqueline Roche

He points to a gorgeous girl in a short skirt.
He asks, "Why are you here with us when you could be like that?"
I look, I think, I speak: "Some girls want their war, too, Sir."
He smirks,
He nods,
And we go back to our drinks.

Soldier, Female

Amy Sexauer

She was born female, but raised to survive
In a world where sexuality has no boundaries anymore
She is ostracized by all genders
When the call came to serve her country, it was a citizen that stood up
Not a woman
When choices were given and duties handed out, it was a patriot that
volunteered
Not a female
Every test, every mile, every bullet, every drop of blood
Every sacrifice is somehow weighted less
Every success tinged with skepticism, every failure somehow foreseen
She signed up to give this country her life if needed
Instead they shamed and muted her identity
Then welcome home to men that won't acknowledge you and women that
can't relate to you
Her only truths are that violence is pure and her duty was sacred
Her only family is a brotherhood that asks her to give everything
But will never have her back
Some men hate her because she has seen behind the curtain
While some women hate her for what she saw there
She found purpose in a team at war, where silly details fall away
Where competency and survivability create bonds stronger than blood
But once that war had ended, all those silly details were heavy once again
Service and sacrifice diluted by pissing contests
How ironic that a soldier always craves a battle to be won
After a clean war, she was blessed with a dirty one
Stumbling awkwardly between the identities and stereotypes put on her
She is wholly woman and wholly soldier; there has never been any difference
to her

Of Fields Unsullied

Caleb Taylor

Sweating through fields of poppy and wheat,
Clambering over walls and the Cross-Canal Leap,
Now into the nexus, the maze of compounds,
Twisting and turning, strong smells and stern gazes,
Words of warning, of caution, despair,
The field is poisoned, none dare to walk there.
Warnings refuted and care cast asunder,
Plunging from cliff with fellows in tow,
Into a sea of unknown, of fear and of death,
A sea of unknown for glory, and the rest,
Trudging on with heavy feet and damp socks,
The objective at hand, the sea is now known,
Field of loneliness between those cared for,
The danger once hidden, newly uncovered.
Caressing fingers trace lines in her sparse green locks,
Now sweeping and probing her damp, brown box.
Poking and prodding now show me your secrets,
A disturbance within, anomalous features,
Buried beneath her like tumors, malignant,
Abruptly bursting forth with a cacophonous violence,
Ripping from life and limb, shattering silence,
Gnashing and gnawing in one great shout,
Primordial scream of terror and doubt,
Dust, debris, and flesh strewn across the sky,
With one great flash a world forever changed,
Buried beneath her, foot soldier's bane.

Contact: The Valley of Debris

Ben Fortier

The endless miles of red sand—
Kicked up in clouds as the convoy weaves
Its way through the Valley of Debris.
The spotter notices an unfamiliar object—
It wasn't there yesterday,
Or the day before.
Swerve, swerve.
The tires lose grip as the trucks lurch.
Throttles roar as the bomb explodes and
Tears off the rear quarter of the second vehicle.
Truck one stops hard and the security team dismounts.
Truck three is trapped.
The Commander is not a patient man.
No follow up.
Eyes are wide open.
Corners are scanned.
They feel the scopes of snipers on them.
The tow bar is finally attached.
"What took so long?"
An annoyed voice over the radio.
They got lucky this time.
His lack of gratitude affects morale.

The First Time
John Dailey

The first time there wasn't time to be scared.
From telling a joke to taking a life
Inside the space of a minute.
The first time there wasn't time to think.
Rifle to shoulder, red dot to center mass
Practiced ten-thousand times on paper.
The first time, time slowed to a crawl.
I watched it all, somehow,
As if from a great distance.
The first time, when it was done,
My heart raced like mad because it still could
And because my buddies' hearts still could.
The first time was different from
The times that came after
But the heart racing always followed
Because it still could.

Abas Ghar
Adam Holroyd

Every step upon the Ghar,
Was one step further from who we are.
Every breath we were allowed to breathe,
Was borrowed time, the price was steep.

"You can't save them all."

You Can't Save Them All

Noel Sadac

We were told
You can't save them all
It was repeated
You can't save them all
I told my guys
You can't save them all
When my guys died
I told myself
You can't save them all
It's hard but,
You can't save them all
You do your best but,
You can't save them all.

A Stone In My Heart

Rob Chmara

Your skin feels like burnt paper.
Last words like ashes,
Eyes like sand.
Zero, this is Three-Two Bravo...
Dead leaves in water,
Floating in a wadi.
Smoke, thicker than air,
The gasping breaths of a dead LAV.
...standby for nine-liner. Over.
Lingers, floats, curls and spirals like a spirit,
Over the ghosts of ourselves we left behind in a grape field,
Twisted and wrecked like scarecrows in a wasteland.

Devastated Dreams

Paul Oliger

The sun, effulgent, through the haze burdened sky.
With terrain as rugged and tough as the lives on the mountain side.
Razor wire stacked high from imperialistic machines.
And a great many people who will never achieve their dreams.

The Grisly Truth

Ben Fortier

A vicious fight ensues in a city halfway around the world.
A dilapidated building houses a gang of insurgents,
Taking on a team of heavily armed Americans.
Close quarters combat. Rifles going off inches from their targets.
The fighters are racked with concussions.
Ears ringing. Adrenaline spiking. Hands shaking.
Engulfed by the fog of war, an American shoots his friend in the back of the head.
Simultaneously, a grenade goes off,
And the dead body shields his compatriots
From the thousands of pieces of searing hot shrapnel.
A lull in the fight allows the men to drag the body
Out of the kill zone.
There is no time for sorrow.
The enemy is still in proximity.
Another several minutes are spent attempting to flush the insurgents
Out into the street to be gunned down by a machine gun in a fixed position.
Finally, the rifles fall silent.
No one can understand how it came to this point.
Everyone is still in a state of shock,
Coated in a thin layer of dirt, sweat, and gore.
Lighters flick and cigarettes singe.
What lie could they possibly concoct
To make it seem like they didn't kill one of their own?

The Call
Danny Robertson

It was down to me to make the call
Hang a left, at that next wall
Didn't see it up ahead
Hostile intent, a ghastly debt
It would be paid, though with a fight
But what If I, had made a right
The burden mine, heavy it weighed
Sudden shock, the debt is paid
In the rubble, there he laid
No sign of life, his cammies frayed
A painful scab, was here to stay
Picked every last, Monday in May
Expecting wife, was at the mall
Oblivious to the pain
Of the next phone call
It was down to me, to make the call
It was down to me, to make that call

Somalia's Fallen Mentors

Greyson Snell

Steel blades spinning above slicing through the sandy air,
a bloody battle scattered below.
A metal carcass plummets to the earth.
The Mog swarm like rabid dogs,
circling the corpse, salivating for western blood.
Gordon and Shughart descend into the dusty fog.
Into the desert warped unknown fray,
the brothers stalk through the rubbled expanse.
Lead riddled fighters' shudder to their grainy afterlife, shooting, moving,
communicating to deaths dance.
Round after round, the end draws nearer,
men, women, children, circle - scrape for the taste of foreign flesh.
Swarmed and devoured, their selfless sacrifices echoing through generations
—just hold on a little longer brother, it's Blackhawk Down.

Eyes Wide Shut

Chris Mattingly

war seems so far away
washed and tumbled in our head, it will always remain
far is a word anything but
never forgetting the souls and eyes

friend or foe, you will always know
when you see the corpse
blood and life ooze away from that mother's child
you know what it feels like

holding her tight i felt life
seeing the carnage that I have committed
knowing that i was the end of her little creation
her eyes always penetrating my mind

her flesh and blood put to one side
cant keep that life from pouring out
holding her tighter than a cravat
I put on a tourniquet yet impracticable

blankets drawn over her brother
eyes wide shut he saw the light
knowing she will be at his side soon
never knowing nor forgiving

we gave no mercy in the parricide
both parents, doing what i would do
showing love, not seeing the death we brought
brother and sister holding each other in that life less way

keep these out of my mind i ask
the sights and sounds
on that rainy and overcast evening
the family was on its way to the prayer

not just these eyes i plead my case
many others have suffered from jihad of the crusaders
many other boys have been bystanders, spectators, or even the athletes
that committed these memories that will always haunt us

i walked into a situation there was no escape
after being blown to the ground by death seeking rocket
boys in shock and speechless
I saw him, ED....was his name

funny around the crew and admired by his wife
not too funny anymore, twisted in that shape and form
half turned over and wet, insides were out and out were in
spanky soaked to the bone, eyes obvious of disbelief

pulling the poncho back i could see
there was no life left to give
these scars can't be patched
seeing the brother that had your back

now never moving off his
memories will always remain
dragging, towing, heaving his lifeless body
is the weight of eternity

help us forget and them to forgive
pray to whatever god that will listen
show him that we knew no different
ask him for the indulgence of peace

Battlefield Playground

Jeff Gravel

There is no more playing dead.
No getting up after a count of ten.
These kids won't laugh or learn again.
They're little pawns in an ethnic cleanse.
They must have prayed
These victims of genocidal sin.
But no army came to aid,
And no adults kept them safe.
They were left alone and betrayed.
When the grown-ups come to play
The war game's rules change.
Hide and go seek turns to escape and evade.
Terrified. Afraid.
And so fucking brave.
Being hunted like prey
Slaughtered in rage.
Below the swing set they lay
Left out on display.
Degraded. Raped,
Shot. Stabbed. Grenaded.
In a massive children's grave
Lie dignity and innocence to rot in decay.
Embraced by the Earth, kept safe in her clay
Six feet below where their little ghosts play,
Far away from grown-ups and their war games.

Red Wheels
Chris Petkas

It'd been a hurry like all else in the way of swaying wheat. A case sat open
with scars like a burned boy able to move his eyes. The eyes of it, the
wheels, peered back with stuck-mud colored in red. I dropped what was in
hand and stared back. All anyone could remember is rolling over life's blood.
How had I walked over it without thinking back, then? So I sat in the next
room and remembered what happened to that burned boy and I understood
that it would have to be alright if it happened to mine.

You Were Always Me

Julian Seddon

Nameless you are, but famous to me. Just a kid, a causality of war
Is what you are. You were nothing to me, until you waved at me.
You looked at me, without a thought of your next step being your last.
You were flying over me like a comet heading into the empty abyss.
You were just a kid—a man in utero.
I didn't know you from goodbye to hello, but we would
Become connected for life. Crossing the rugged road
With that famished cow, you two took off
Like bottle rockets aimed for the glass dome, piercing beyond earth.
I watched you from a distance, step on that hidden stack of destruction.
The moondust covered roads where our paths would cross, led me to you.
I could have never imagined that a quick split second could make your loss
More a part of me, than my own skin. For your cow had even changed forms,
It was now a blasted meat stew mixed with metal twisted in a tree.
I ran to you, or what was left of you. There was virtually nothing.
Your death is now my war waging inside of me. It kills me to know you died
For me. If you didn't exist, I wouldn't be able to write these words for you.
I owe you
A life, the one that you missed because you hit the road like a bouncy ball. A
road meant for me to meet my maker, instead you became my vessel sent to
the sky for the big sleep.
The afterlife, for you may be different.
You are just a dead kid whose life fragments were embedded into my boots,
skin, and soul. You are the reason I am here. We were always meant to be
me.

In This Place

John Dailey

In another place you'd be in school or on your way.
In another place you'd be thinking of girls, or cars, or sports.
In another place it would be a baseball bat or a fishing pole over your shoulder.
In this place it's an AK, and you're a "Military Aged Male."
In this place, through my scope, I can see both fear and resolution in your eyes.
I pray you get to be a kid in the next place.

A Poem:
Tamim Fares

I think about him sometimes, in between the dull
thoughts of the day, like "what shoes am I going
to wear," or "I wonder where I can find the best
deal on grass seed." In those moments, when
the neurons go slack and lazy, when the mind
sinks into itself, that's when I see him as he was.

I push the thought away, unwilling to yield the
prosaic pastures of my mind. Unwilling to see.
But of course this is folly. With every attempt to
forget, his resistance increases. Red and Laughing
in the face of my impotence. There is no escape,
no relief from the crushing truth of what I've done.

But why should I feel bad? He knew what he was
doing after all. "Wrong place wrong time" they said
and shook their heads in commiseration. First, the
Captain came and took my statement. Next, the
Chaplain came and took my spiritual pulse. I spit
and laughed, bravado on my face, ice in my veins.

Afterward, I smoked my first cigarette, and then a
half dozen more. Searching for something in the
haze, something ineffable that was long In coming.
I was congratulated, patted on the back and passed
around. A shining example of the ruthless killer
instinct they were trying to cultivate.

I see his black shirt, his yellow sleeves. The small
backpack, bouncing as he crosses the road. But
more than anything, I see the Red wire clutched
in his tiny hand. It trails behind him, snaking around
piles of rubble in the road, disappearing into a trash
Choked ditch. A dog is barking somewhere.

I do not hesitate. It would be easier to say I had,
but I did not. From my hidden perch I watch him
Take his last step, then the crack of the rifle, the azure
blue of the cloudless sky, and he was gone. Swallowed
up by the Earth. Another windswept day in a forgotten
Corner of the globe.

Motherhood
Jacqueline Roche

I almost died for my daughter.
So much went so wrong,
Even before she took her first breath.
I'd give my life for hers,
That's not a question.
Years ago,
When I was just a girl,
I watched mothers hold their daughters close,
In order to entice others to their side,
And then blow themselves up.
I hold my daughter close and wish,
I could have been their mother, too.
Engulfed in the fire of a mother's love,
Rather than the flames of a mother's madness.

Little Girl in the Purple Hijab

Heather Kaiser

Mud walls, mud floor, mud crusted on your feet,
Stained into your yellow dress as though it is part of the pattern
The disarray and darkness inside
No beds, just a carpet, scattered items, utensils, clothes
Everything smelled of mud, and worse...so much worse.
What was your name?
Memory is failing...
What were the names of the other children in the village where you lived?
I think often about you and many children from over there,
It has kept me up on guilt ridden nights alongside other nightmarish truths.
You were so innocent
I think about how you smiled for me when I asked to take a picture once,
You had no idea why...but maybe you did
You are one of the few of whom I have a clear picture,
Posing with your headscarf.
Your mother was so kind
Eating vegetables and tea with you, your brother and mother – sharing all of
the little you had,
Trying so hard to solve unsolvable problems, bigger than both of us,
I'm sure you were probably confused as to why I had so many questions
And why I was even there in the first place...you made me feel like a most
welcomed guest.
I was so humbled
for having so little, you smiled so big
for having so little, your mother was so generous
for living amongst the dangers, you were so resilient for living in those
conditions, you were so content
Where are you now?
A sickness fills me when wondering whether or not you're still alive,
I promise to never take your photo down, so you won't in my mind
Your smile, the wet mud, your mud hut with the broken, rusted tank carcass
near your front door,
Frozen in time from the last war—I'm sure those soldiers remember your
family too.
You help me find joy
Most times the abundance in front of me makes me ill,
You saw so many painful, awful things
You had nothing, and were still able to smile
When I think of you and it makes me appreciate everything I have now.
I pray that you are alive and well, still finding reasons to smile
Little girl in the purple hijab, I thought I was helping you, But you were the
one who helped me
You made me see the world in a new way
What a gift.
I only wish I could have made life better for you.

Over the Radio

Noel Sadac

Over the black gear we get the call
We run to the ECP
We see a family
A kid is hurt
We smile and treat her as family
We hope she remembers us
Because that is our legacy.

The T-Wall

David Curci

You find out what truly matters
In this world
When you cover another human with your body
In what you believe
Are the last seconds of your life
In hopes that he might live
Instead of you

The Analyst's Regret
Simon Paul Burke

I knew you once,
but now you are gone.
A good man died,
because I was wrong

Tracers
Mike Swart

Lightning bugs,
Lightning bugs
Moving so fast
Come out to greet us
After the blast
Buzz like a zipper
And sting like a bee
Whose stinger is lead
And terrifies me
We call out for dragonflies
Who circle above
Spitting out fire
With the most hateful love
Complexity
Next to me
Side of the road
A nest full of hornets
Set to explode
Butterflies,
Butterflies
Safe landing zone
Tell us we'll make it
Carry us home

Pedro (9-line)
Lauren A Campbell

Dust-flecked blood, darkening skies
Racing, chasing death
It's just earth – peppered with lead
Scarred with strife, marred with loss.
"Fifty feet, doors"
That grit in my teeth, familiar dust in my lungs
Another son on the dark edge
Hanging on under that smoke, our siren song, calling to us:
Bring him home.

The Storm Has Come / The Field
Theodore Harrison

Savage children
Unwashed sons
Cold, hard ground
"take us home"
"the storm has come"
But trans is late
So, you're fucked
My son
Fat Major
Clean Major
Come to see
"help us sir"
"the storm has come"
Sorry hero
We're not your ride
But hunt the good stuff
Climb to glory
Take it in stride
Warm Major
Gone
The remnants of us
Wait
That's not our convoy
No boats to the other side
Clean phantoms
Stare,
And fly by
Please
Take us home
No
Are you crazy?
The storm has come

Helpless

Mike Swart

Kill.
Why do you remind me
You didn't pull that trigger
You gave the command
Light them up
Waste those motherfuckers
I see muzzle flash and movement
The Ma Deuce thunders a wonderful song
It's not enough
Call for more
Bring fire and death
From a squad eating lunch
Reading letters
Listening to peace songs
Help us
We feel helpless
There's more to life than living
There's dying.

The Trees Were Green, Until One Wasn't

Julian Seddon

Animated green reflections that radiated off the trees ate the finely grained moondust like we did.

But those deep seeded trees never seemed to be one with it; not yet completely blown into the sand:

This road was long, rocky, dusty, narrow, and small. Berms jutted from the earth shadowing to the east and to the west the road folded down into the earth molding into the wadi and then raising up on the other side where it folds back, breaking, and crashing down once more with that familiar adjacent long, rocky, dusty, narrow, small road.

A small foot bridge made of tree limbs bonded by a mixture of mud and straw stretched across the wadi, connecting them for life. Those two sides will always be together; however, in this space of togetherness—everything fractured. Broken bodies we were, expended into the materials that encompassed our universe. Leaving one piece of ourselves behind everywhere we go, adding to the trail of souls that were depleted or already deleted. We are leaving a footpath until we are empty - empty as empty could be. Unfortunately, emptiness hides the matter that takes up its space. Fucking empty. Try again: nothing is ever empty.

The road was like an open house, deserted, but setup for a purposeful design. And then...

I saw him. He saw me. He waved to me. I waved back to him. He smiled at me. I smiled back. He was the heart and mind. Longitude and latitude were about to meet; about to make coordinates. It was a sacred sector that we would or should have crossed paths on. Little did we know, the man in dark blue was waiting, hiding, and ready. I'm sure his heart was beating fast, but we didn't know. I'm sure he has done this before, but we couldn't be sure. I'm sure he knows he fucked up, but we know he doesn't care.

The connection was proper. From a single button. His remote was successful, except—

The timing was all wrong. I knew this because I could hear the thunder, I could feel the debris pelting me, bouncing off my flak, and even sticking to me. The heat, the smoke, the sand all embodied me, and then came the deafening silence it discharged. The dirty freshness we didn't see is now the wretched that we are provided.

The man in dark blue disappeared as the remains of that long, rocky, dusty, narrow, small road became larger than the universe. The ground was ruptured—the ignition that was meant for me, made that innocent disappear into the atmosphere. Only fragments were left to pick up the pieces.

The leaves on those trees still glistened, with lush greens; all gleaming, expect one. It is now bare, bruised, blackened, and broken. Eaten by the sand. It stands alone remembering the mistakes that were made transforming me into the tree that never blossoms.

Shaken Not Stirred

Nicholas Gaines

Do I feel a pulse?
Not amongst the gods of war
Achilles, Hector where have you gone?
-Within-
The people say the war "God is Dead" - Nietzsche
The people? Our people? You people.
Frozen, lost, divided, and burned
Swirling around the Devil's stick in the cauldron of division and hate
-Lost at Sea-
But what of us? Are we lost? Never. (We're right here.)
Our path was written in blood, a map, a compass
Forever etched in the sands of the desert floor
Afghanistan, Iraq, Syria...this list goes on
Flip the pages and read our names between the weathered bindings
And when the last name is read
-Do I feel a pulse?-
The war gods beat their drums
Back home they will never know
Back home they are lost at sea
Round and round they go, where they end, they do not know?
-"Remember you will die."- (Says Marcus with a smile.)
We've been here before
Our path is straight across the river Styx
The boatman greets us
We've been here before

Seasons Change

Anthony W. McEntee

I remember the warmth of a young love, like the summertime, bringing a sensation of a thousand butterflies; joyous and optimistic.
A naive soul, not yet jaded by reality's cold embrace.
I survived through the fall, and though the warmth is fading,
I still look to the heavens, hopeful and patient.
But now the winter has come and the landscape is barren.
I watch the last leaf of a dying tree dance its way to the frozen ground.
My only indulgence is that of the flesh.
A lust fueled feast; an attempt to satiate my starving humanity.
I seek reprieve for my wicked ways.
A gust of wind, the aroma of gunpowder on the breeze, a boom in the distance, all remind me of my younger days.
My stomach grows warm; a flutter of monarch wings.
I smirk with hollow eyes and fade into the ether, as the boatman quietly sings.

Follow Me
Arlene Hidalgo

He's uneasy, his thoughts pacing as he moves away from me. I call him to come close, his attentive eyes shift to avoidance, I remind him that there is no place for fear in our wild hearts. I turn to face the threat and push forward, he trails behind me, ejecting any hesitation, he executes at once. Our bodies collide in celebration, his spirited gaze restored in victory. Hungrily, he awaits our next opponent, formulating his strategy to gain ground. He trusts me blindly, I hold that high and I will defend it.

She is My Girl (Ode to my 40)

Zachary Aloysius Burgart

The way she holds my hand, like a young child eager to explore the world, clinging for my comfort. I needed the comfort too, I always have, even before I knew her. The way I know the position of my fingers, on her rings, her familiar grooves and edges. I know she is there for me, she always will be, because I take care of her. I know she is a strong girl from the way she has bitten me, she has hurt me, but the love comes back. I'm always the first to apologize, I clean her, I treat her delicately. The way she rests on my chest, the way she rests on my cheek, the way we fit together. I always know how full she is, not from the subtle differences in her weight, but from what we have been through together. I love letting her eat, I keep track of what she eats, I miss letting her eat. Letting her cool off, following a hot and heavy experience, where we both maybe got too excited. I love that she lets me dress her, that she doesn't try to change me, but I really miss how quiet she is. Unmistakably most of all, I miss our conversations, with friends from afar, It was never about me, it has always been about her, And that was perfect.

A MOTH FLIES LIKE A RUBBER STRIP CHARGE

Mike Murphy

From the Lions Den
This moth deserves more than this
Dying slowly
Stuck
A black rubber mat with no feeling or soul
A black rubber mat that is perfect for a ribbon charge

Let it go
Fly
Fly again
To life or through a door

Sick Call

Nate Yake

I went to see the doc
To have him fix my ailments
And cure all my afflictions
I asked him for some pills
And if he'd write a prescription
I explained to him the tragedy
Of how I started out strong
And the day that came too quick
And where it all went wrong
I begged him for a cure
Even considered surgery
But alas there were no treatments
To fix my broken humanity

EXIT ONLY
Rebecca Monaco

Islam is the way that I am told is true
The important thing is to reach the roof
Then why are the pillars collapsing beneath
And this prayer rug pulled from my feet
Declare your faith, pay your alms
And pray that your sins have gone
In the crowds, the West rebels
But they'll be silenced with a single shell
Withhold your tongue of disbelief
Or your life will end with greater grief
Now cover your face, say your prayers
And strap on this vest if you so dare
Your time is done, just accept defeat
Pull the trigger, and God you will meet

Invaders
Danny Robertson

In these sins, I relive
Hope for blame,
Objective
Loved ones laments, shattered cries
Sandbags hide their frightened eyes
Take your strong
Make them weak
For your sake, I hope you speak
Invading thoughts, in the night
Pending souls, pray we're right

Ridgelines

Nick Rossin

We stood shoulder to shoulder on those ridgelines when the world was at its worst.
Only the truth at the bottom of each man's heart would shine through on those moonless nights.
When men are forged, and cast into a brotherhood that no God can match.

Time
David Hartmann

How much time you got, Yankee?
It's called your Forever War.
I don't think that means what you think it means. I am Afghanistan, lower
Persia.
Forever is longer here.
Welcome, sit down, pull up a rock...let's talk.
I'm glad you invaded, '01, what a year.
Now two decades passed, those black turbans still fester.
Will you stay? Will you go?
Again, that "F"...word, is it apt? Is it wrong? That word..."forever" Only history
will tell.
When we lack you foreigners,
we just fight ourselves.
Masood, Northern Alliance, Dotsam, Haqqani, it just feels wrong when there
is no Afghan killing.
Before you was Russia
with their red stars and tanks.
You taught us to fight them.
Here, your cold war was hot.
You gave us Kalashnikov and Stinger
to fireball their choppers and mortar their faces.
I thank you for that as we now mortar YOUR bases! Back then you thought
us friends,
but now this century...we're not.
Before them were Brits.
Their Light Brigade charges. Kabul, Kandahar, Ghazni,
Our blood mixed in all.
I was part of that "Great Game" Between Russia and Britain.
A game played with lives, treasure, blood, and will.
That's my kind of game, indeed.
They carved up the globe.
My border they drew.
Only on paper that border exists.
My people don't care.
They live where they live and fight where they fight! We don't use maps.
We don't see lines.
We are trails, tribes, and strongmen. Our lines are in our faces, not places.
The Brits didn't learn.
Britain invaded at least twice.
That's right, you cheer beating them once with flags, bangs, and beer.
I celebrate anniversaries
of breaking their will
TWO times per year!
Many an Englishman still lie in my sand.
To their credit, still now, they jump
at the chance to lend you a hand.
Whispers of Empires are a lure few can fight.
How will your grandchildren judge your time here? Maybe they'll be here too.

Send them, I'm game.
The Mongols, The Huns
Alexander, his Greeks,
way back to Darius.
My mountains, my deserts ran red with their blood, my sky held their shrieks.
All came with a plan
that seemed just and sound. Most bled, all wondered, where they'd lie in my ground.
To me you are ALL vagrant.
You are temp, you pass through. The Army of the month.
I age in centuries, how old are you?
Your decades seem long,
but they're a blink in my eye. I've been here before you, I'll still be here after.
I am Afghanistan.
Forever is longer here.
How much time you got? Nothing is forever.
How much time you got?
I bet I have more.
How much time you got?

One Year Puzzle Pieces

Mariah Smith

Again and again they asked us to go
For the duration
In one year chunks
We fought the war one year at a time
And I lived my life that way too
A different person every year
One year home and one year away
I reinvented myself every time
It was easy to do
necessary even
This time I was a bold platoon leader
That time I was a stern XO
Another, a shrewd planner
Or I tried to be
Driven to be what was needed and serve in the manner required
My payment was a piece of ribbon
A living wage I couldn't spend
On a life I was absent from
But also priceless friendships
Invaluable lessons
Exposure to the world
At 'home' I was many one year things also
Always knowing I'd leave again
That time was too short
Not all of them lasted
But each one became a part of me
Built me piece by piece
For a long time I hated
this fragmented version of life
Then, like a puzzle
It slowly formed into an entire picture
And I became grateful for all that I had lived
And each piece I had been
And who it had forced me to become

JTAC
Daniel Horgan

Jokester on the battlefield,
Thrown to the wolves,
Aggressive with his vengeance from the sky,
Courageous are his actions to bring the rain.

Anger is for Amateurs

Ryan Friesen

Hardship is a gift
Sisyphus had it all wrong
Embrace suffering

"This might be home."

War Buddy
Jacqueline Roche

War Buddy took my hand,
And walked me into war.
When I got home,
And the war came with me,
War Buddy took my hand,
And helped my heart come home.

Forward
Cody Ford

Bullet broken bones
Healed but the deep scars remain
Grin and keep walking

My Walk
Dale Rider

Look 360 and pull my security,
I watch everyone intensively.
Footsteps approaching aggressively,
I use reflections to try and see
who is it and what they carry.
I speed up my pace, they pick up their speed.
My heart beat is racing fiercely.
My eyes dart, looking at who looks at me.
My mind races, my feet move rapidly.
This is it, I spin around to meet
who's this foe that follows me.
Except now he crosses the street.
In confusion I now can see:
I'm home, safe as can be.

Why I Run
Jake Howell

It began in the beginning,
In sports and in school.
It was focused on winning
And running was just a tool.
For teammates, for competition,
For trophies and recognition,
      It's why I ran.
I knew where I was headed.
It's about strength and discipline.
Parris Island, I had always dreamed,
Required shifting of purpose and not a little adrenaline,
The pounding of boots, the singing of cadence,
A new identity, completing the distance,
      It's why I ran
The desert, the sand, the war in Al Anbar.
Distant gunfire, shrapnel marred his body.
We were needed, but a little too far.
Mind over matter, it was no longer a hobby.
Not for accolades, not for a score,
We kept running, a little more, a little more.
      It's why we ran.
I couldn't wait to come home.
Now I long to go back.
What was once a nightmare in my bones
Is not a nightmare in-fact.
To be known, accepted, to share the common bond,
I've come to love it and how my heart responds.
To remember... It's why I run.

Outside

Mariah Smith

The thing I miss most when I am deployed is the outdoors
Ironic, because most of any deployment is without a roof
But cages are everywhere
The metal armor of our vehicles
The concrete walls of our FOB
The weighted plates of my vest
That I feel each time I breathe
All the things we cannot do
And the hard things we must
To restore myself later
Whenever I could, as much as I could
I galloped my horse across the winter cut field
I plunged my hands into the garden earth
I slept beside the campfire, safe on my own farm
My worst foe a copperhead or black bear
I fostered tiny orphan kittens
Moved to tears by their determination to live
I breathed in the smoky light of fall
And realized the year is a wheel
That brings me back to a new type of wholeness
Outside

At War With Myself

Ben Fleming

Chased my dream and volunteered for war,
Not quite the gap year all my friends went for,
Won't catch me listening to those fear mongering bores,
I'm a twenty one year old boy who knows it all.
Careful what you wish for, it might just come true,
Seven month adventure, just simply get through,
Said "hello" to Terry with a round or two,
They played a good game from my point of view.
The chaos, the destruction, the barbaric action,
Hellfire's, Machine Guns were one amazing distraction,
I paid no attention to any compounding reactions,
My mind left addicted, craving another chemical transaction.
War had given me all it promised,
It was everyone back home I found most dishonest,
Sure there were things I'd rather have not seen,
But I'd found a home in the big green machine.
Blessed to come home without a scratch,
But that's when it all started to come unpatched,
Life at home and war so incomparably mismatched,
My anger could be summoned in just a flash.
I fucked it up for all who could see,
A kid, a girl, a job just wasn't enough for me,
It wasn't money, possessions or wealth that fed my greed,
My adulteress was war and she refused to leave me.
Like all stories of life the chapter passed,
Spent more than a minute as an outcast,
I changed my perception of what I encountered,
My experiences in life have helped keep me grounded.
Whatever has happened to you in your past,
The darkness that follows can be surpassed,
You've all seen the films where good always wins,
The trick to happiness is you have to let it in.
My soldier mindset was my limiting belief,
Stuck in a time because it made me feel so elite,
So I wished that part of my life farewell,
And set off on a path I call At War With Myself.

First Shot
Timothy Falke

I can remember how I felt that day,
The sand in my eyes as the helo flew away,
I can still hear it, my weapons boom!
Shoulder to shoulder we cleared the room,
First shot, body drops, blood is on the floor,
First shot, body drops, point man through the door,
Second shot body drops, you are forever changed,
Second shot, body drops it starts to feel the same,
Third shot, body drops, war leaves you wanting more,
Third shot body drops, civilian life's a bore.

The Sea, It Pulls Me Back

Joe Bowling

I thought myself a traveler here beneath your waves.
Tides teeming with life, bearing relative to my own.
World before my world,
skewed through a single filthy lens.
Unwilling or unable to fathom
the scope of your primordial reach.
Anchor chains take hold
against the current of common sense.
I no longer fit the mold of a man that treads on solid ground.
Stomach turning and twisted into knots,
I long for sea and salt and home.

Homecoming

Neville Johnson

Dimly lit empty room
My life boxed up
My war over
Feeling empty
Feeling numb
It's over and done
White noise breaking silence
There's no joy
No contentment nor despair
Unable to think
Unable to feel
A void filling my empty soul
Numbness consumed me
Filling me to the brim
My war is over

Today is a Good Day
Lauren A Campbell

Every day I step out, I'm going to die.
It's an old familiar friend by now.
Never alone, me and my demise.
It's not that I plan to - want to.
Every day, good or bad, I've come back.
Others haven't, won't.
Days filled with gunfire, radio static, shouting
Nights with accuracy, tactics, immediate actions.
I don't flinch anymore.
I think they trained it right out of me.
A steady hand in combat
That shakes at home in bed.

Residue of War

Nick Misiano

Talk about war
Open Pandora's door
Study lessons in warrior folklore
Or just eat yourself, inside-out, forevermore
But that's just picking at scabby, puss-filled sores
Boring you with gore
Fallujah corner store
Demolished in a down pour
Steel rain for the Corps
From ship to shore
Kickin' in your fuckin' door
My Dawgs just shit on your floor
Dirty, sick, and poor
No empathy anymore

The Long-Leaved Flowers Weep

Emilio Gallegos

"There must be some kind of way outta here
Said the joker to the thief
There's too much confusion
I can't get no relief"

"All Along the Watchtower" – Jimi Hendrix

It saved my life, English Literature
And I'm not even sure, I knew it then
But when Tennyson spoke, he awoke some
Thing in me, and I could see heavy ink
While I was sinking, further into my
Chair, and the air seemed eerie, wearily
Reading a long, to the song of men, sweet
Music, of tir'd eyelids upon tir'd eyes,
And I realized that there is in fact,
Confusion that is worse than death, trouble
On trouble, pain on pain, he was saying
What I was feeling, silently reeling
In this newly foreign place, struggling
To embrace the disgrace, of not finding
A way to say 'I'm OK," and mean it.
There is confusion worse than death, I know
Because it snatched my breath, sped up my heart,
And part of my left eyebrow disappeared
In 2009, everything wasn't
Fine, and I trembled in my sleep, that was
Something she didn't keep, from me, and while
"She" isn't important to this written
Collection of words, she heard me groan and
Jerk, while my mind worked, eyes closed tight, struggling
With another fight, still at work in me.
The charmed sunset linger'd low adown
In my red west, and it would come and go,
The pain in my chest, I wanted to run
And run, and run...to nowhere, and stay there.
Tis hard to settle order once again,
Or remember when, my insides didn't
Feel so bizarre, always wanting to drive
Myself to the ER, flying over
80, north on 280...I still think
About dying, when I'm crying on the
Inside, eyes wide shut...somewhat, blind to the
Fact that depression is real, and constant
Regression will steal your joy...and destroy
You from the inside out. I'm inside out.

Lines

William Bradley

The lines around his eyes aren't from his age
They're from anger, bitterness, and years of pain
At 22 years he's seen his share, and he'll never forget his brothers that he
left there
In Sangin, Afghanistan, his youth he there left
A place only a few understand, the Valley of Death
The crack of the bullets is a sound he won't soon forget
Nor the screams of the wounded or the silence of the dead
Hunted by the enemy in that lone, silent field
Danger was with him, the fear that was real
Through the smoke and the hell he emerged as a man
Leaving behind him a trail of blood in the sand
The bottles he drinks, he hopes will suppress
The demons that surround him, memories he'll never forget
He relives those nightmares every minute of the day
Sleep is no comfort, nor prayer that he prays
Because the horror that he's seen at his ripe tender age
Is etched in his memory, in the lines on his face
His time there is over, at home he now reflects
Of the four years of life he gave, and this, he doesn't regret
But those lines around his eyes will forever remain
Constant reminders of the hardships that he's faced
The death of his friends, the mutilation of others

Are the reasons for these scars, wounds that remain uncovered
Faces of the men that he killed, the child that he saved
Will stay with him always as he lives out his days
Life he has given and life he has taken away
Guilt resides with him, and himself, he will always blame
What none will understand is one simple fact
That those lines around his eyes are battle maps

Z-I-H-L
Samuel Raymond Santry

After All,
It's a Smokey Old Lounge
a Bitter Brew helps
a Few Friends understand
Grab up a matchbook,
Strike up a Conversation,
REMEMBER the days when we brought that Middle Eastern Sun to its
Knees.
Burn up some more Tobacco.
After All,
It's a Smokey Old Lounge.

A Beautiful Abomination
Evan Reichenthal

For me, this was my new life.
I heard how the others hated their new bodies.
Nothing could prepare you for this experience.
Doctors seemed confused by my acceptance; it was abnormal.

Yelling could be heard with regularity in these halls,
Our situations could always be worse, they said.
Unclear of where I go from here?
Reality is what you make of it, or so the saying goes.

Perhaps I could go to college?
University was always an option.
Righteous indignation was all the new rage they said,
Perhaps I won't fit in with the university types, I'm not a victim.
On the outside, I looked like an abomination of flesh and metal.
Somehow, I found peace with my new form,
Even monsters can be beautiful.

The Painted Face

Anthony Severo

It started long ago
A war movie, a TV show
Being a kid all I wanted was to wear camo
It came to fruition when I was eighteen
Those days when I was lean and just a little bit mean.
Though only a few times I felt as though something was finally mine
Among the dirt and the bugs, the paint on my face was more than innocent fun
Now far removed or so I thought I struggle with the hardest battle I've ever fought.
The paint on my face remains, through the daily scrubbing and the shaves.
Walking through the lecture halls and sitting in class no one should ever know.
I do not want them to know.
To be found out would further darken the line, not a single veteran shirt is known to be mine. I have not found any common ground but I dare not quit to become a statistic
It always happens when I pass them on the sidewalk.
Their eyes only on their phone, they will never know how it feels to be truly alone
A painted face, just wanting to be home.
Should one look up, they find a regular face with a quick smile.
They always look away shy and I do not know why.
Can they see the paint? I thought it was only me.
Sitting among them, I am unburdened and yet so uncomfortable.
I do not want their weighted blanket they bought online, I already had mine.
It was laden in MOLLE and the smell, not so jolly.
Every day I wake up I wish to be clean but that greasy paint cannot be unseen
The painted face is who I am.
I am the painted face.

Education Benefits
Ryan Friesen

Don't say much in class
Exchange canteen for Nalgene
Soldier ink displayed

GI Bill

Joshua Sooklal

As I wonder where life has taken me
I assume the worst
What did I do?
To be getting free tuition

Ghosts

Javier Rodriguez

So what was I supposed to do?
I had a choice and I knew it. I was surrounded by people that had it all
figured it out and took me 20 years or so to realize that none of us had
anything figured out. I wanted to impress people, I was young but I wasn't
stupid. I just had a fight and a grudge in me. So I left it all and flew away to a
land that didn't know me, a land full of fire and heat. A land I was supposed to
hate but didn't. Now I'm a father, a husband and the ghosts I have haunt me
a little. Not much but sometimes they creep up out of nowhere. Creep up and
out of the musty basement I put them away in to die. I see them when I go
down to do laundry, when I check the furnace and when I need a spot to do
push ups to get rid of this belly fat that's been bothering me lately. I know
they'll always be there. I chose them and they won't ever forget it.

Hard lessons, but I don't regret it.

Bad Man

Anthony McEntee

They say home is where you lay your head
But I won't know where home is til I'm in the ground, dead
Cause my soul is restless, always on the move
and The wind on my skin, keeps me nurtured and soothed
I walk these streets and I dance in the sand
Just to love a good woman, and to kill a bad man
I have seen the sun rise across the world
And I've broken the heart of more than one girl
Cause my spirit is fleeting, beating for the road to unfurl
As the sands of time, spiral and swirl
I walk these streets and I dance in the sand
Just to love a good woman, and to kill a bad man
The pistol is cold in the dark
But it's warm when it's workin, when the lead hits its mark the life drained
from his eyes
A reflection of heaven, now he stares at the sky
I walk these streets and I dance in the sand
Just to love a good woman, and to kill a bad man
I wear these lines in my flesh
scars of age and from chasing down death
My soles are worn thin, and my soul is damned
Cause I loved the wrong woman, and I killed a good man

Pardon Me

Brian Straub

Pardon me,
I'd just like to get by please
Without remembering
Without forgetting
Without being torn apart by the two
I just want
To get through
Without the pain
But, with the pain
And climb
I just want to make use
Of my time
Out of respect for those that no longer have it
Who lost it by being in the moment
Can I please
Just be in this moment?
To be useful
To be remembered
To not be tired of this life
To be measured only by how much I loved
And was loved
Pardon Me
Not to be judged for my mistakes
I have paid
Not to be placed on a pedestal for achievements I have made
They are not for you
They are not for me
They are for them
So pardon me
I'd just like to get by please.

Hey Hero
Michael Baumgarten

Hey hero, did they tell you the price you'd pay?
What did you buy with your life?
Did you save the day?
Did the ones you love understand your time away?
Hey hero, why did you walk away?
When they thank you, why do you flush with shame?
Did you find enough tombstones?
Can you remember all the names?
Hey hero, do you sleep ok?
How do you keep the nightmares at bay?
Can you still see it the same?
When someone gets too close do you push them away?

Hey hero did you cross the bridges you burned?
Do you talk to the others?
Do you hope they're concerned?
Hey hero, you're going the wrong way
Didn't they tell you about the pain ?
The thoughts you'd have that ask to escape
Does it all make sense?
Have you found your place?
Is the world less bright than it used to be?
Do you love the same?
Have you found peace?
Hey hero it's ok
Have you asked for help?
Did it help anyway?
Hey hero, do you like that name?

Cell

Roman Newell

Had no way out
so I went in deeper;
they gave me a knife to cut my own throat
in the:
con c cell. r ete
I chipped away at the walls until I could
taste rainwater
dripped from
petals
of tired flowers
plucked by boys
in a place called Helmand, in a place called Panj'wai,
trying to find beauty in drizzle filled skies.
I climbed out the vagina of damp earth,
WALK,
below the prison, another rattle,
the snake strikes then slithers away,
burning hail greeted me;
it said:
the outside is no better,
it told me: the foreigner
is a part of our jihad now.
It's hard to breathe
but as long as you can choke you can breathe.
machine gun fire, warmth, explosion, warmth,
lazy snowfall,
slap my face again
so I can shake the shivers, slap my face-
slap!
Again, again-
SLAP!
Put me to bed, put me to rest,
REST?
A bulletproof vest
does nothing
but make better marksmen of your enemies.
Deployment marries eternity.
Reconciliation,
putrid smell,
and the smell brings the sounds
of devastation,
and the sounds of devastation
bring the smells of fuel and ash and carbon and burning rubber and burnt
flesh,
and the smell brings the images
of blood and severed arteries

and helicopter MEDEVAC,
and the images bring fear,
and the fear brings sadness,
and the sadness brings the drink,
and the drink brings the cocaine,
and the cocaine brings the numbness,
and the numbness brings the devastation, and the devastation brings the
con c cell. r ete

IT'S A RAID

Roman Newell

The fight is colossal inside, it outgrows the body,
a vermin eating out of the belly,
trail of blood around me,
I tow my shadow with a UV light,
trail of blood surrounds me, wagon wheel formation,
a bold man
with a bold plan and a circle of trust
always brings more blood.
Boiled blood boils out protein,
water is the only change,
like a good woman
no one sees her next to the warrior,
but without her
the blood does not work.
Men of oil
conflict with life, men of oil separate like dark and light.
We slip out when the eye's lid
has shut.
The soldier leaks into the dark night
from the dark hut like a murmur,
articulating through fields, over rooftops, down alleys, like a dying sergeant's
breath.
He delivers a whisper and a kiss,
a letter with inked fingerprints and seven droplets of blood,
Fucking war
makes sex in bed to dogma,
Congress is only ingress to foreign lands,
Fuck 'em,
pulsating piano sticks,
all soldiers carry a riddle, all soldiers have their
burden.
We pay upfront for honor and repay loans
for dignity,
brothels of politicians replace
brotherhoods,
open a knapsack
inside of a backpack,
withdraw a bag of pills
and a bottle,
infiltrate the target's premise,
gun to his head,
I'm looking down a barrel,
IT'S A RAID! IT'S A RAID! IT'S A RAID!

Things I Don't Tell My Family

James Freeman

solace always starts within arm's reach – quickly dispelled the things felt,
known, are forever bound
sweet twine tied round my stalwart heart
that which chokes also saves, makeshift stitches
along bleeding fault lines
the smell of poverty, corrupt air - third world burnt oil breeze slick and
comforting, a sigh of relief - yes yes this might be home rubble strewn
streets, curious sights, who left this hand here
why would tea cups stand true, unbroken, alongside people shattered living
in moonlit splendor, the world rendered green and black, pixelated action
dances across sighted glass, red lines tracing for release like hellbound
hounds feed me feed me, grant me purpose, calm fingers locked
endorphin rushed caffeine mixers, serotonin cocktails chase tobacco ladened
highs
this might be home can you feel it?
the deep spined need for an opening shock, promising a few minutes more
draped in the sky, burning in burning in, mustn't waver
bleeding footprints showing where you came from, imperious brow pointed
where you are going - always forward
the thrill the chase the opium promise of gunsmoke adrift acrid pavlovian
drive painted black below my right eye
the constant whir, a dominion of panasonic background noise, silence
splintering never truly settling around you again, silence knows you are
marked
for shouts, decibel splitting dirges of shrapnel and haphazard cyclic fire
the overpressure- kinetic, real - upon your being
hear the whip, snap, joyous full hearted shout of metal hunting flesh feel the
sharp flaring flame, body battered against man made machines
dance to the tell-tale whistle of random chance raining down
each laugh measured, each smile worn - trenches hold the best actors
this might be home

"It's only a dream once you wake up."

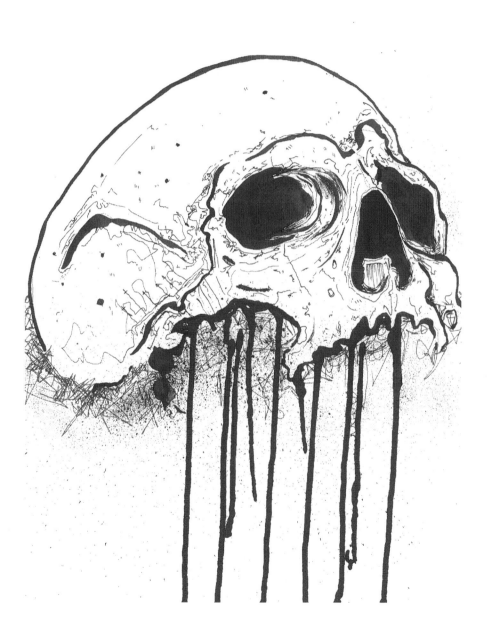

I Slept in Uncomfortable Places

Luke Ryan

I slept in uncomfortable places
Rocks were my pillow
I slept under a blanket of cold sweat and matted mud.
Restless was my body, stretched thin was my mind.
I slept where things were jagged
Where the midnight storm would wake me
Only moments after my eyes fluttered closed.
I slept with thunder in my mind and lightning to the north.
But since I have returned to the pillow,
To the blanket and the warm body next to me.
I have not slept so well.
I have not slept so well at all.

Dreaming
Samuel Raymond Santry

What was it really?
Was any of it real?
Does it exist now as I remember it from then?
I think…
It makes no difference.
The world keeps right on moving.
While my dreams are still fighting the war.

In The Middle of The Night

Tim Lyons

Returnfiremake'emhurtboysohSHITjohnson'shitthegroundreturnfirekill'emallg
oddamnfuckin'ha jjisWax'emMEDIC!
Johnson'sdownHe'stalkingnonsensebleedingrealbadDocHeneedshelpwhatar
eyougonnadol'vegotaMEDEVAConthewayDocgimmelines3,4,5thebirdneedsit
NOWheyisHegon
namakeitDocwhat'sHedoingHeneedshelpweneedaMISTDocwhatthefuckhapp
enedwhy'dHeclose hiseyesheyyouGOTTAHELPHIMDOC-
Stop.
Watch the ceiling fan spin.
Slow down, breathe out then in
Feel the sweat on your bare chest.
Look to your right and see
Her.
Grab her hand gently, she'll wake up
Slowly
Things will get better.

GREEN MONSTER
Rebecca Monaco

Through these lenses, the world is green
Abstracted reality, seen through a screen
Just another short life on loan
Like my NODs, I'm government owned
The moon has sunk, the night is gone
But green blood still stains my palms
The sun is up, day serene
Skies are blue, but my world is green
Scrub my hands, wash them clean
But underneath, they still feel green
No time to feel, can't stop this machine
But deep inside, my heart beats green
I fill and drain my G.I. canteens
But in my mouth, I still taste green
No night of sleep will set me free
For even then, I dream in green

The Night Bus

James Freeman

the night bus is always late
i sit at the stop - Via Cassia is quiet for once
odd... it looks like i'm heading home?
surely making curfew is out of the question
but thinking on it - where exactly am i coming from?
i grab the dwindling pack of chesterfields from a pocket - light one quick
hoping the sultry sweet smoke sorts things out
looking out and looking in - my sight grows dim and features fade this stretch
of street exists alone
burning quick i draw one more - i pause, hearing a bus draw near
N-25? its doors open - it never passes through here
out he steps, so familiar, and deftly sits beside me - what could he possibly
be waiting for? tail lights disappear - i go to light another, the red bic flickers,
flails, dies
turning towards the other i ask - hey man can i grab a light?
a quick negation - nah don't smoke, you can bum a lip though
he passes me a green tin can - wintergreen, my favorite
wait...dip? i've never...
feeling ice cold fingertips, slick with familiar scent - i look up and finally see
him it has been years - you could have told me, you know?
i can't breathe, i watch as his face changes, each one so damningly known,
until worst
i don't recognize them - the dead yet to come
his face returns and he repeats - you could have told me, you know?
i back away frantic, looking down i see my skinny jeans replaced by torn
Crye cammies
seventeen, but i feel the unkept beard against my neck and distant ringing in
my ears this was never Via Cassia. this can't be real - you could have told
me, you know?
tell you what?! it's all i knew to say, all we were ever taught, the ole "don't
worry, buddy you're gonna be okay" - fearful words, the last you wanna hear
because it is a death sentence in disguise - it didn't even need to be spoken,
i'm sure you could see it painted plainly in our eyes
he sits silent and i return beside him - i'm sorry im so sor-
hand raised swiftly, cutting me off - i know - he says- sad smile set
for so are we - he grasps my shoulder
and i'm there again waiting for the ambien and everclear to do the trick,
another thing you aren't taught - how to sleep through the day after a night
like that - counting each incoming siren from my cot - gnawing question
stands, how am i still alive? a question that persists until...well, it doesn't-
there is nothing noble in this art, only a carnal truth remains - all we desire it
to come home unsung or undone - two masters, two certainties held tight,
swimming below the caustic fervor we so willingly embrace each night - you
can have one or the other, never both - and as these things go, you're never
happy with the fate you know.
headlights approach and i snap back - the N-25 once more?
he stands to leave, as do i - to follow

he pushes me back - not just yet - forearms clasp in a final farewell and the bus moves on
face shaved, hair long, everything as it was an easy numbness settles in
i'm definitely missing curf - no wait, this has happened but it isn't now
nor was that then and here again, surely i must be dreaming? checkered vans kick the dead lighter across the street
forgotten in hand, blood smeared - the tin oddly alluring
muscle memory kicks in and i find my bottom lip half full and i swear i can hear the radio checks as the birds spin up
i sit at the stop - Via Cassia is quiet for once the night bus is always late
it's only a dream once you wake up

Homesick Dreams

Stan Lake

I dreamt about you again
With your age-old violent sand
blowing above desert scrub-lands
And groves of lush green date palms stand
I felt homesick for your dysfunction and death again
I grew sick in my dream longing to see them,
my brothers now scattered on those arid Arabic winds
Time, distance, and change are all you are to me now
Like a warm blood-soaked blanket on a cold night you comfort me with your trauma
I miss the frightful nights and boredom days
I long for the camaraderie and sibling rivalry
and the shared disdain for our big Army family
I always wake up missing you
and feeling like I still owe you
As if I haven't done enough for your cause
Because my brothers kept the fighting going on
Years after I left to go back home
to my other life, The "normal" one,
or so I thought
years and miles removed
Who knew the real war wasn't in that distant dirt but in the memories,
in the restlessness,
in the hurt.
Wipe the sleep from my eyes
and feel the creak in my knees
I'm home now, no longer overseas
The truth is that I've been homeless since I left you.

Mind Games

Dale Rider

Vividly and violently
I remember every eye I see
Wildly and widely
My brain drains silently
Heavily and heavenly
I dream of death defiantly
Casually a catastrophe
Rest for me or rest in peace
Finally I'm Fiery
My deep scars are my diary

When The Guns Fall Silent

William Bradley

His heart is heavy with the fact that it is over
He yearns for his war, like a faraway lover
He lived for the fray, and engagements he won
But the battle he can't win, is the fight in his soul
For he lived as a warrior in a far, distant land
Cutting his teeth in mud, blood, and sand
In the streets of Fallujah, the poppies of Helmand
His soul was there taken, the Devil's forever
He can't let go to this craving that lingers
No drug can compare to this vixen's soft whisper
The smells of the powder consume his mind daily
Like the scent of a woman, a fragrance addicting
Closing his eyes, his body is reminded
Arms are now heavy, from the weight of a rifle
Strain in his shoulders from the mass of his plates
Hands closed to fists, clenching grenades
He looks to the moon, and remembers a night
When it's great beauty chose to delight
In the view of Marines, alone in the corn
Tracked by the Taliban, hungry for blood
The only regret he has of that day
That the enemy left, not wanting to play
For they would have died.
And much they would suffer

Screaming in pain, crying for their mothers
The sight would be ghastly, blood filling the earth
Another faction of evil to rot in the dirt
A flurry of wind blows hard as he waits
His lovers hot breath caressing his face
He looks to the sky, stomach is churning
Birds blocking the sun, the reaper is flirting
In the belly, he sits, awaiting his fate
Fear shredding his nerves, sweat drips from his face
Their wings pound resounding, fury their veil
They fall from the sky, descending to hell
A legion of rifles erupt as they hover
Their cargo unloads, searching for cover
Like wars long ago, men fight with a passion
To murder their rivals and reduce them to ashes
The war there is over, and at home, he wanders
Empty of joy, no feel of belonging
Heart of a killer, his fingers now tremble
Itching for one last pull of the trigger
Blessed with a family and land full of peace
No more could be asked for, no more could one need
But the love of his wife, and love of his children
Will never equal the satisfaction of killing

His mistress now lies with him in his dreams
The soft kiss of death interrupts his deep sleep

A snap of a bullet, an explosion so violent
Interrupts silent nights with blood curdling cries
The warmth of her breast burns hot on his chest
Like the hot desert sun, alive on his skin
Lustful desire fills him inside
A fervor so great, he will never deny
Years have gone by since last he embraced her
He longs for her body and soft touch of her fingers
Senses are heightened, he will always look back
Searching for one last thrill of combat
The love that they made, time cannot erase
Sweet was her presence, violent her ways
With blood on his hands, he always will wish
For one final taste of her luscious, red lips
At night he wonders if she thinks of him still
But as he drifts into darkness, her voice will be there
For when the guns fall silent, he listens and hears
The war screaming his name, his lover's sad wail

Gremlin

Alex Horton

I met the leprechaun
In the green suit
With the funny hat
The pointed black shoes that curl over three times at the top
And the pot of gold at the end of the rainbow at the age of twenty-four
Now, I realize, you really never should meet that fucking guy that young
He pulled back the curtain too early
And gave me all the psychedelic chocolate I wanted
While forcing me to watch as gremlins attacked the wings of the plane I was
flying in
I couldn't steer and I just had to hold on for the ride
For the longest time
I thought I'd be chasing that fucking asshole for the rest of my life
But now as I look back, I know you can only eat that chocolate for a short
while
And you'll never kill all the gremlins
They only eat at you
One must shake his hand one last time
Accept all the cavities
Overcome the withdrawals
And eventually find peace in staring at the rainbow from a distance
Instead of blaming it for all the darkness in this world
It takes a long time
And I'd say, I'm only halfway there.
But I no longer miss that green suited fucker
Now, I smile and remember his laugh
And his torturous ways
But I no longer wish to chase him under the green haze of night anymore

Searching Senselessly

Noah Hoglund

Sensible searching senselessly
In a wrap of moral decay
Running around restlessly
In hopes to find a definite way
The roach of remembrance
Which kindles like an ember
Calling on the lost, defiance
In the autumn past September
Watching dreams float down
The maple sheds its colour
And in the crippling sound
Thoughts pursue another
What is the desire of the past
To arise admirably amidst all
In search of a passion, alas
Slow down and answer the call

"The best we can do is etch their names onto a rock."

Memories in Stone

Luke Ryan

I meandered through ancient stones in a newborn land
There is history here,
Chains torn by strength and flowers wet with tears.
All these lives, bursting onto the earth in passion and flame
Growing and sleeping and laughing and weeping,
And the best we can do is etch their names onto a rock.
And yet this place is soaked in their lives,
And I will let my soul marinate here for a while
Like a man parched of memory, granted a few treasured drops of water.

THE BAND
Zachary Aloysius Burgart

The band is playing again.
I'm excited.
I'm nervous.
It feels like it has been so long since we've seen a performance. But I think they played last week.
Everyone is here together.
This band has the best set list.
Simple man.
Yes.
I love this song.
I'm people watching.
They are happy to see each other.
I don't think I've ever seen them before.
There are more people here than I thought would come. I don't know why those people are here.
They didn't know him.
I don't think they care.
Oh man.
The band is playing so well.
They are really crushing it.
They are playing with so much passion.
I think the singer is crying again.
I'm crying too.
I start to stare off.
Staring at the poster.
The boots.
The rifle.
The helmet.
The dog tags.
Yes, the band is playing again.
People are starting to get up.
Say goodbye.
Instead of leaving they are going to the front.
Like a communion line at mass.
It's my turn.
My knees are weak.
My hands are shaking.
My knee touches the ground.
I touch the cold helmet.
My eyes closed.
Images of him flash before my eyes.
The last images I'll ever have of him. He's gone.
Struggling to stand.
I return to my seat.
I holster my pistol.
I sling my rifle.
I go outside.
I go back to work.
The searing desert sun.
And the band plays on.

Black Band

Jeff Gravel

This black band around my wrist
Has your memory engraved.
With every pint that I tip
And each whiskey that I take,
With every embrace that I give
And each hand that I shake,
You are not forgotten.
I'll tell them your name.
I'll speak of your deeds
And the life that you gave.

Section 60
John "JT" Tysver

60; just a number to most.
However the 60 I know is in this Virginia field.
A land of stone rising from the green grass,
A place of sorrow and mourning.
I come here to visit my friends with a six pack of beer under my arm;
Like the days of old when I would walk across the grass to a buddy's barracks
With speed so I wouldn't be late to our deployment sendoff party.
But here there is no music blaring,
No shouts of profanity, black silkies revealing pale legs and tattoos to accompany, And the random grunt donning nothing more than body armor and a gas mask for the night of debauchery.
I recall these memories and smile as I make my way through the mazes of stone.
I find my place in between you all,
And I crack my first beer.
Section 60; our post-deployment party begins.
Here's to you Boys.

(Section 60 is a piece of Arlington Cemetery, roughly 14 acres out of 624. It's most notable as the place where a lot of the people killed in Iraq and Afghanistan are buried.)

Roll Call
Charlie Martel

Your family isn't here yet, nor are the men selected to stand by you on this day. It's just you and me in this cold room with its high vaulted ceilings. I slide a ribbon back into place, fix the angle of your crossed arrows. They did a good job dressing you.
I wipe a minute smudge from the brass with the back of my white glove. I say your name quietly to us. The next time will not be so easy.
The chaplain is here now, reading your coroner's report to me. I'm not exactly sure why. We all have our ways to cope. Maybe that's his. Even in death, you are Army property and both shockingly and unsurprisingly an officer needs to sign for you. As glad as I am to have him here with you and I, his reading is starting to feel like a third wheel. I'm holding back emotions I don't feel validated in having. You didn't know me well. You didn't pick me for this job. I was selected by the clock, being your sergeant major at the time of your demise...and I can tell you nothing in my training has ever covered this. "....a bullet entered", I concentrate on your gig line. Your family will be here soon. I'm glad there are so many of them. There is strength in numbers. But your wife and daughter...they have become my liege, and nothing I can say or do is going to make this easier for either of us. Part of me envies you. Whether you are looking on or are just gone, you don't have a speaking part today. I'm going to do my best for you brother. Not just today in this ceremony that you would complain about dressing up for, but for as long as I breathe. As long as I have a voice, it will be for your family. I swear this.
Your teammates are here. The Praetorian Guard ready to form a phalanx around your loved ones. We wheel you into the main chapel. I adjust your flag, draped over the lower half of your casket. One final look, a spot of lint on your Beret plucked away and I leave you to conversations with those who need them, deserving of your last minutes face to face.
Your friends and family have spoken. The Ballad has been played. Pipes screamed your name. And now it's my turn. The part I had to be ordered to rehearse for timing...I call the name of teammates past, the name of your team sergeant from Afghanistan. "Here Sergeant Major." I don't know how they sound so strong. I call you by your rank and last name, the name the Army gave you. I see the rigidity in the Green Berets standing at attention before me. I call your name again, adding your first name. Shoulders are tensed, faces steeled against what is next. I call your name. Your full rank and name. "Ready! Fire!" The report rips through this crowd assembled to see you on your way, an invisible bullet piercing our hearts. It fells your wife. I've shut myself off at this point. It's my only option. I need to make this work, for you, for the memory that those who love you need to take with them. The casket is closed and your flag drawn over like a blanket. Quiet marching commands, and small, crisp movements of your Praetorians. My hand extended, three seconds up, three seconds down. I secure the hearse door with a firm but quiet click.
Your teammates and I stand by, stoic as you depart. Unsure of what comes next, but ready for it. I guess that's on me.

Arlington (Home Again)
Lauren A Campbell

I'm tired and well worn, less Rockies,
More Appalachia. I'm sitting on the floor-
A room with a hundred doors. I can't even find my keys,
My body betraying me
I'm just there, sitting, searching
All options, no means, just reaching.
Which door is yours?
All these rows of rounded marble memories.

Section 61
Thomas Schueman

Virgin and bare –I wait
For those that fall in fields of folly
Impregnate my fertile soil
I swallow seaman and soldiers alike
My forbearance wanes
An insatiable appetite insists: Feed me your young
The best you have
My neighbors feasted
First-course Pork Chop
Second-course Hamburger
Dessert is mine
A fresh arrival from Helmand
Special delivery from Dover
Promenades of The Old Guard
Percherons pull a caisson adorned with a casket
Glory! Honor! Duty!
Revered in death
Expendable in life
The wait is over
Chaplain benedictions
Holy invocations
A mother's lamentations
Final roll call
Private First Class Schmitt
Private First Class Eric Schmitt
Private First Class Eric E. Schmitt
Honor the dead
Fold the flag
Three-volley salute
A bugle plays Taps
Shovels sling clumps of dirt

Strands of pearls,
Crowned with wreaths
Section 61: Grave: 1
Inscribed epitaph: Loving Husband & Father

The Soldier

Hugh McNulty

I was a soldier once, I was.
I was a father, a son, a brother, someone's heartache, I was.
But now I'm a number in a line of white, a Commonwealth headstone
shimmering in the French sunlight.
I answered the call, I stood up and took my place, and here you are now
staring tearfully into space.
You visited me and stayed a while; you cried a little but I also saw you smile.
You're proud of me and those in this line, we will never grow old for we've
had our time, but don't you fret old soldier friend of mine.
I was a was, but now I am an I am, for you don't see the grave you now see
the man.
I am a soldier again on the line with them all, awaiting what will be our last
bugle call.
But as you leave there's no need to remember my name, merely go
home ....and tell them all.... the reason that you came.
Humankind - be both.

Terra Nulus

Moises Machuca

Betwixt us is wedged too much mediation.
Our commonality is estrangement.
Self-preservation's our liquidation,
The universal fungibility,
Flag draped coffin, there's the commodity
There's the brow laid low whose self is private

There's sameness between high rank and private
We belt-feed the culture's mediation
Thus, induce our own fungibility.
Freedom, we judge it a commodity
On trial and guilty of estrangement.
Go, drink from the cup of liquidation.

Empty ego's well of liquidation
Why do you keep your past veiled and private?
SGLI says ima commodity
Money exchanged for a life's estrangement
Coffins as boxes, our mediation
Same different forms of fungibility.

The screen manifests fungibility
Washed and reified for liquidation
In step with each day's task, our estrangement
In place about-faces mediation
Life's hustle and bustle keeps us private
To compete against your commodity.

Exchange for use value commodity
What's our use now post-fungibility?
The war bored with us gives mediation
A thanks for serving, now keep me private
Life does not live in liquidation
Nor does it know itself in estrangement.

What seems to be strange in our estrangement
Is our consumption of commodities
To alleviate swelling of private
Anguish. Yet, we produce liquidation
In love for war. Our fungibility
Is your entertainment's mediation.

Too much mediation found in private
Our estrangement turns to commodities
Liquidation of ego through fungibility.

Broken Barrack Box in the Basement
Jeff Gravel

Old maps and cam creams.
Ripped gear with tattered seams.
Cleaning kit. Canteen.
Bug dope. FMP.
Nightmares. Can't sleep.
Box of ghosts and memories.
Compass mirror. Same me.
Wedding photo. Shattered dreams.
Letters from her. Wasted ink.
Broken heart. Back bent.
Pain pills. Pension cheque.
Broken homes, no picket fence.
Greener grasses with dead ends.
Dead watch. Time spent.
Drunk again with dead friends.

Ice Cream

Ryan Kisner

Done with deployment now; back home.
Friends are outside going about their lives. It's cold.
Family is near me, but distant all the same.
I'm eating ice cream through cigarette breath.
Alone in my room.
With my gun and some plastic spoons.
A bottle of whiskey too.
I know I'm home.
As the eventual sweet release I feel is akin to sodomy.
Sweat, blood, cum, tears.
I am home in fear.

My Cave
Nathan Nash

And now I retire and escape to my cave
Where it's cold and dark – my living grave
Where the outside world can't feel my rage
All my loved ones safe at bay
Behind a door and curtains that hide the day
Alone in my head I wish the world could see
A mile in my boots through Nuristan and a sit-down with Chai tea

The Night I Tasted Brittany

Matthew Horning

Cold hard steel
Bitter taste of carbon and CLP
All my demons fighting
Alcohol's not helping
This is the only solution
I want out
I'm throwing in the towel
Drop the mag
I have one in the chamber
5 pounds of slack
Then there's no going back
I can taste freedom
The answer to my conundrum
Breathe in Brittany
Paint the walls with my epiphany
I'm sorry
I have my finger on the trigger
I couldn't do it
God dammit let me do it
I hate myself, my life, my being
A blur is all I'm seeing
Am I a coward for not taking the coward's way out
I have the rest of my life to find out
A life I now live with open eyes
I am a new man
I know that I can
I still have problems
But never will I go back to rock bottom
Like I did that night when I tasted Brittany

"The remedy, to the longevity, of recovery, isn't easy to come by."

Recovery
Simon Paul Burke

How many men have come as close?
How do you fight "the quit"?
How many men damn near overdose,
when "good enough," isn't?
How many men, are drowning pain
deep inside the bottle?
How many men, chase feeling whole
Wide...open...throttle.
How many men are empty shells?
Just spent casings of war.
How many men now find themselves
not who they were before?
How many men now, just exist,
going through the paces?
How many men, awake at night,
remember anguished faces?
How many men struggle to live,
haunted by so much death?
How many men...suffocating.
Alive but without breath.
How many men worry and fret
struggle each day to see?
How many men, forgive themselves?
Then why can't you and me?

1-800-273-8255

Greyson Snell

My brotherhood of blended men
A family of different blood
Birthed by the mother of adversity.
Conflict is the air, that fills sucking lungs
War and loss, our soulmates
A lustful hunt, breathing purpose into our lives.
Lives, dreams, personalities - donated to liberty's cause
Faces forgotten, muddled, erased in the flesh
Some of us, defeated by our minds captivating darkness.
This group is small, lethal, yet breakable
All are needed, depended upon... cherished
Keep pumping red life, do it to your utmost.
These brothers and sisters need you
The ones that fell before, beg of you,
Live and die for our family - we did.
[Don't you ever give in]

Group Therapy
Chris Wilson

Anguish and obsession
reveal the hidden lesson—
if we're receptive
to learning and growth.
I'll share my experiences
while trying not to choke on
the rock in my throat.
Language doesn't offer
the words to describe this war,
but every two-weeks
I'll try— just a bit more.

The Absolution (Pantoum)
James Moriarty

I will not surrender.
Myself I do forgive,
I will ascend in splendor.
I was meant to live.
Myself I do forgive,
For unforeseen mistakes,
I was meant to live.
Now this just raised the stakes.
For unforeseen mistakes,
I do appreciate.
Now this just raised the stakes.
It will never be too late.
I do appreciate.
I will ascend in splendor.
It will never be too late.
I will not surrender.

The Fog, Wins

Emilio Gallegos

The remedy, to the longevity, of recovery,
Isn't easy to come by.
And I've often asked myself why,
Does the sky shine bright, why
Are cumulus clouds such a comforting white,
And why, can't I sleep comfortably at night,
And why, hasn't this fucking fight
Ever ended, why, have I pretended
That I'm doing great, and feeling fine,
When nine out of ten days, are clouded
By a haze of numbness, and my left ear constantly rings,
And the things going on in the left part of my neck
Reflect the tension in my brain,
Or at least that's what my mind is saying,
To myself, during these almost daily talks,
When walks out of my apartment feel like stepping off to a mission,
And the transition from Sergeant to civilian,
Feels like a million needles pushing through the heels of my shoes,
When the heavy days come in twos, and threes,
Choosing to seize, the day, or carpe that diem,
Gets lost in the shift from AM to PM,
And here I am again, trying to begin,
To separate the victories from the sin,
And spin around, in my own private mirror,
To get a clearer, picture of the grace on my face,
Standing in place, struggling to fully embrace,
What I see in my reflection,
Because this moment of introspection,
Carries the heavy weight of expectation, and personal pride,
Tilling the cold soil of toil, and hot desert sand,
My left hand goes numb, and my right squeezes tight,
And despite hours of therapy, and pages of stuck point logs,
The fog, wins.

Breath

Amy Sexauer

Warriors in training
Tied weights to their ankles
So they could walk
The ocean floor
So disciplined and strong
But they forgot
How to take off their weights
And
How to breath
On the surface

30: A Reflection
Bryan Crosson

Circled the World twice; Been in gunfights, knife fights
Bar fights; Climbed mountains, dived oceans;
Been right, wrong, loved, lost;
Won't quit till every
Drop is squeezed
From this
Stone

Do Not Mourn My Passing
Justin T Eggen

Do not mourn my passing
For it was a blessing
To know her, to meet you, to greet him
Everything has an end
Death graciously gifted a life worth living many years before we became
entangled
Limited time to enjoy the warmth of the sun
The cool of the night as the wind fluxes across my skin
Embraced by loved ones in genuine admiration
These are things I have tried not to take for granted
Death reminded me throughout my life that I would be taken
Not Today
Were the words that were spoken
So many times I've had my life bruised & broken
Many more times the pieces were collected & mended
Failure is not failure when I learn and adapt
Failure is progress and progress is learning
Freedom to learn and grow my mind
Freedom from toxic destruction
Death has given me some sort of reasoning
Some sort of instruction
A blueprint to live fulfilled, to live strong-willed, a life where every second is
slowed down to dissect, digest, & instill
Particular patterns in my mind of memories allow easement into the unknown
Do not mourn my passing
For it was always bestowed

The Sliver of Sun

Luke Ryan

I met an old man,
'neath a tree older still.
I asked him from where his wisdom had come,
"Not by my hands, or by power, or skill,
I ran, I ran to the sliver of sun."
"The darkness is strong", he whispered the truth,
"Courage is born through the broke and undone."
For the sake of the light, he gave up his youth.
He ran, he runs to the sliver of sun.
"The young are naïve, the old seem forlorn.
You carry their weight 'till the race has been won.
You run through the night, for the old and unborn.
You run, you run to the sliver of sun."
For fathers, for mothers, for daughters, for sons,
I run, I run to the sliver of sun.

A Sunny Day
Chris Wilson

A sunny day
through the windows—
beaming in with blinds closed.
Peace outside—
war in mind.
Cut off from the outside.
Isolate no longer,
war monger.
It's a new day—
fire away.

Final Knell

Roman Newell

For a moment I feel strong
as though the souls
of all my lost mates are in my bones, for a moment
I feel strong melancholy
like I've been
stripped naked for Patricians' entertainment.
A beggar tells me my soul looks worn.
The mind is not so different from the body;
the deepest scars
run like Iraqi ditches
and our legs
sink into the mud.
We are mollified then forgotten.
I need a kiss somewhere deep inside but men don't kiss men, and they are
all I have in this desert
with donkeys,
and sporadic gunfire,
I am home,
I am the safest
thing they have,
but the most
dangerous thing I have.
They write promises
on scrolls
tied with yellow ribbon,
halfway to heaven they let go
and you fall.
Home is tired, home is numbness, I tried to kill myself in a car,
I tried to kill myself with pills,
I tried to kill myself so they
couldn't do it first.
I was tired of getting gifts from people who
hated me.
Only those who
have never researched death
call suicide cowardly.
The more you understand something the more you respect it.
It's why professors
speak reverently and explorers over-prepare.
The blood fills the pool. The blood fills the bath. we're all craving
the best sleep
we've ever had.
It's always the places where we can get most lost
that we feel the most found.
Funerals and wakes
are the parents of the forgotten dead;
eulogies and classifieds are their grandparents. I'd write a list of all their
names,

but they are many,
and nobody wants to be forgotten.
Brothers-
I'm most tired
when it seems the only way to forget some of the absence is to lose more of
them.
You go from a kid
walking down the center of the street with a cigarette
because you're cool
to a man
walking down the center of the street with a cigarette
because you don't care if you die,
and I lean back
in this messy bed smoking a cigarette
while the American flag out the window,
across the way,
sits silent,
like it too is frozen.

We Are Always Going to Die

Ryan Kisner

Traveled often enough;
I bought Dramamine repeatedly.
Used it often enough;
It may have killed some better parts of me.
Vicarious violent tendencies crawl through my mind.
Usually it's when I'm standing in a goddamn line.
Just waiting around to buy some more cancer.
Take 7 minutes off my wretched life with each fanned flame.
People see the ink that's been laced by my own stain.
Self-deprecating thoughts in my brain.
Moving in and out like fucking waves.
Withdrawals are motherfuckers, I'd rather have none.
But I'd keep them all the same.
All at once.
Need caffeine in order to run this machine that is me.
Nicotine too.
Mild states of euphoria.
Brought on by items listed above.
Add violence.
Add objects.
Not people, objects.

The Cog
Michael Tribbitt

Yellow footprints on a humid summer night.
Heart pounding, fear of unknown through the doors to our future.
13 weeks to tear us down and build a better version.
Become a warrior.
Stories of front-line battles turned to day to day fleet regularity.
Countless training missions in climates that mimic a battlefield you will never visit.
Promises never kept
Medals never earned
Thanks, given for service
Sitting on the bench during the championship game
A game you never played
Understand that you are a part of a machine.
A war machine
You served your purpose.
The chapter was written.
Finish your book.

The Millstone
Chris Stowe

The millstone blocked the head of the stream,
choking off all life, all feeling, all dreams.
Its weight – immeasurable; a behemoth in size,
blocking all emotion, all memory; even life as time flies.
The water it rose and it fell; it crashed and it lapped,
behind the massive millstone, all things stay trapped.
Downstream from the millstone to the horizon lay wasteland,
the hardpan stretched for miles, the lone work of my hand.
'Till the day the cries downstream, the din too much to bear,
compel the hands that once placed it, to now turn and tear
out the decayed millstone with the effort of Atlas;
the time it has come; this water must pass.
The men and the missions that created this stone
will forever be loved and revered,
but it is time to go home.

Of My Old Life
Matthew Sabedra

There are times where I find myself missing war
Not for the adrenaline rush, the promise of glory, or the sense of adventure
I miss it for the camaraderie and the sense of being a part of something bigger than myself
The long talks of philosophy, love, loss, and life with friends over cigarettes
Making memories which will last a lifetime

Ghosts of War
Simon Paul Burke

While once young, and full of breath
I've watched the exit, a turn to death
A pain surreal, and yet we bore
Our brother's gone, now ghosts of war.
I have observed, good versus bad,
who fought with all that they had.
I've seen these two equally achieve,
the pursuit of their common deed.
We've killed each other, and to what end?
That we have both avenged a friend?
A holy war, we both are fighting.
Both of us will end up dying.
Long before the task is achieved
We will never get relief
I fear this war will carry on
Far after, you and I, are gone.

Restoration

Cody Ford

I hold something in my hands
That was once imperfectly beautiful,
But is now broken
And put back together.
If I stare long enough
And hard enough
And with enough love,
Will the pieces of my heavy heart fuse
And become whole again?
If I carry you far enough
And hold you tight enough
And with enough strength,
Can my bullet shattered bones heal
And become unbroken?
If I pray deep enough
And clear enough
And with enough faith,
Will my war weary soul
Ever find its way home?

Pulchrum Quidem est Bellum Gerere

Moises Machuca

I have loosened the tight tourniquet
That has swelled my conscious with remorse
To spill freely over to imbricate.

As a bit curbs the spirit of a horse
Impregnating man with domination
Over fellow man and nature through force
Done in the name of God and nation;
So have you tightened your grip on the reigns
Of the other's and your own perception
To excuse your role as bringer of pangs,
And as the defender of freedom,
To do anything else and you would deign.

O, Calliope, I am from Adam
Thus, I have reached the boundaries of my speech
If you judge me a most worthy alum
And wish for my words to fly-high and reach
Do not hold back now but be my mouth-piece
To say what has been tamed and breached.

O, you valiant warriors of peace
You who have mistaken life for lust
And have piloted home from overseas
A war we all must share; one that will rust
But hope it burns-out. Your love for life
Is so great that you feel as though you must
Take another's to preserve yours. Thus, strife
Is exchanged for life and you are left alone.
And so, you take solitude for your wife,
Cemeteries and bottles for a home,
Friends and family for a mistress
No commitment lest from you they were formed.
Still, wage war in freedom's name, the empress,
So your children may know a life with war
And appreciate a coffin dressed
With colors that all others abhor
For there is no room in the circumference
Of the earth for ideals foreign to yours.

TRADING PIECES
Anthony Russo

I live with a puzzle that I'll never solve. How am I so calm, accustomed to it all?
They laughed at me in my father's clothes, His shirt to my knees.
They're all better than me I suppose...
I thought this was the bottom till I watched it all erode.
The green Durango I now called home,
Which led to that time I couldn't act grown.
Screaming as we freed our parrot to finally roam.
I didn't even like him nor he did I,
But now I'm alone & needing a cry.
Where was my mother to wipe these tears,
They don't let track marks into heaven .. or so I hear.
I hoped my fate would change & soon,
But the next day was spent in a waiting room.
Dad's hernia medicine sold fast!
A recovery bed for this man at last!
Still rolling with the punches, back to showing no fear.
Being the troop my dad needed near.
Mostly enjoying the roof & bed for I knew it would disappear.
Many times more I would not have enough.
Many times more I would not be enough.
& on it goes till I just had enough
& my daughter now grows with toys stacked to her nose!
Her reality so opposed to mine that asking for more toys,
in her mind, seems fine.
Aging on an estate with her private trails & lakes
& now I'm the leader who can't relate.
GWOT struggles to empathetically communicate.
Eyes at my feet, standing on a city grate
& all I can see is my childhood face
Handing me puzzle pieces with a look of dismay.
Stretching to reach me from his deep dark grave.
I still hear the echoes of what he had to say:
"These pieces won't fit either but you must know why. If the puzzle is
completed your hunger will die. Keep burying the pain, focus your drive.
Keep the extra pieces to help those you pass by. You're born from the mud to
keep them alive. Their beacon of light in the dark of this fog. Unmoved by the
emotions thats shaken them all. You must carry this puzzle which you never
can solve as a reminder to your unwavering resolve!"

"Today we live for love after the war"

Take Off Your Armor

DJ Sorensen

Come home to me my love
While you are here beside me
You are far away in moments of inner battle
Take off your armor
You need it no more
No bullets nor blade shall pierce your body
Lay down your arms
No longer shall you wage war
Speak freely
For no more will you keep quiet in the dark
Rest your head
Your vigil is over, the watch is done
Close your eyes
I will keep you safe from the enemies at our door
Please come home to me my love
For you are no longer at war

Wildfires
Brett Walker Bender

The glittering leaves of green and white
Cottonwoods on this canyon floor create
Visions of the meadow where
The wars outside me are done
The wars inside me are won
and
With the resting of my forehead on yours
Wildfires of worry within my wicked head are burdened to
Rest.

Today
Nick Misiano

Today we lived and died
We remembered and cried
Today the sun shines for us outside
We reap the clarity of eyes open wide
Today remains embedded in the frontal lobe
We send remembrance in the form of odes
Today we un-shoulder those heavy loads
We recall thousands of footprints in the road
Today we live for love after the war
We let go of reasons to settle old scores
Today a breath is a gift
We rummage through old photos of grit
Today we ran the streets like pirates
We stopped a few times to watch the sun and admire it
Today we lost friends but gained insight
We fought harder than we ever had to fight
Today the darkness returns to light
Today Al-Fajr (The Dawn) erases the night

Unchained

Javier Rodriguez

The city was frozen the day I returned from hell for the last time. I watched her in the glow of the night as we raced through town. It was good to be home. "We have to make a quick stop." She said, I knew where we were going. My mind rushed, how would they take me? Would they like me? Would I be the man I hoped I could be, the one they deserve? I cracked open the window and I could feel the bite of the wind as I watched their little bodies walking towards the car, I took a deep breath. They climbed in and I saw their excited but puzzled faces. No war on earth could prepare me for moments like this, but I was ready. Finally I was there in person, not on a bright computer screen 7,000 miles away like I had been so many times before. They both stared at me smiling, and I fell in love.

Untitled

Phil Sussman

For those we love, we will suffer.
We yell, we brawl, we cry, we embrace, we laugh, and smile. We endure.
We share photos of our kids, stories of our wives, and memories we can't
forget.
We are gods, armed with victory's narrative and fueled by blinding desire. We
are untouchable.
We are fragile. We bleed.
We are 'just tired.' We are 'fine.'
We carry the weight of those who no longer walk the path.
We burn their memory into the flesh of our souls.
We crave a life of worthy sacrifice.
We remember.
We remain.
We fight.

Love
Dave Curci

The right kind of love is not one that I run away from.
I will run towards it.
Like I've run towards the sound of the guns.
As I've approached the door of a building.
The door of an aircraft in flight, still nervous.
Always cautious.
But, steadfast and
With unwavering intent to take on
What will happen next.
Being comfortable with the unknown that lies ahead.

Much Ado About Something

Emilio Gallegos

That keeps bringing me back
To this quiet place,
An unexplainable embrace,
Of nothingness, unless
The occasional sleep influenced barks
And squeals from Samson,
Reveal and chance and,
Opportunity to question
Myself here in the silence
Of my apartment,
And compartmentalize,
My very focused cries, for help,
And stability, forever leaning on
My own ability, to see myself through it,
A conduit, that can never quite close the gaps,
Perhaps, I'm expecting too much of myself
Trying to measure my wealth,
By how many hours of sleep I can muster up,
Rolling my eyes at my half empty cup,
Of despair, sharing,
The deepest parts of me,
With a tiny handful of individuals,
The residuals of 2008,
Making me hate, unsuccessful days,
Because the nonsense stays,
Plastered to my soul, and short-term goals,
Seem unattainable, concentration only sustainable,
By lengthy moments of seclusion,
And as the illusion I create, begins to dissipate and morph into
Something new, I'll take a few, deep breathes,
And push away from the mess,
That my life has become, hiding
Feelings that continuously make me numb,
To interactions and emotions,
Floating in an ocean,
Of doubt, without anyone in sight,
And I'm fighting, to keep
My head above water,
And I hear my daughter,
Say, "I love you," and my son say, "I need you,
To follow through, on all that we've planned,
And finish the conversation that we began,
When I was last in town.
And by the way, I'm coming down,
This weekend, to see you guys,
And surprise sister for her birthday,
And I'll probably stay,
Until Sunday night, if that's alright."

And of course, I'll say, "Ok,"
Truthfully wishing he'd stay,
Forever, and never leave.
I can't believe, I let days turn to years,
Of my children living in fear,
Of their father. It bothers me,
To the depths of my soul, but I feel whole,
When the three of us are together,
And I never, want a day to end,
Without them hearing me say, "I love you."

Untitled
Dan McDonagh

You chose another
So I chose war
Neither of us knew
What we asked for
Two broken souls
Of the same feather
Destined to never
Be together
Teasing the other
Like the sun does the moon
A painful dance
A graceful tune
A song we endure
On our own
Together apart
Forever alone

Fighting Pays Better
Cooper Thompson

i've always said "i'm a lover not a fighter;
but fighting pays better".
and the boys would laugh. i'd laugh, too
irony goes a long way in this job

it's a tough thing to reconcile
being violent and loving
because if you're like me
one comes easier than the other

for me, violence is love
violence puts food on my table
it keeps my children warm
because you can't love a heating bill
into the black

i don't want to be remembered as a warrior but a man's gotta do
what a man's gotta do
so when the day comes
when i've gotta kill
or be killed
just know
i did it for love.

The Boy Knew War

David Rose

The boy knew war.
Exhausted—having played with gun and sword,
He knew before he *knew*—
War was coming.
And, well, it came.
Battlefields weren't just Iraq:
The personal life—
Like most wars:
A series of wins and losses,
Ground gained and moments of terrible waste.
On the other side of it now.
For so long childhood, viewed in gold;
Before it all got so fucked up.
But, gold, not so!
Because the boy knew war.
He knew it was coming.
And, well, it came.

War simply is,
And perhaps that's the only lesson,
When the boys finally the man.
On the other side of it now. Carnage behind,
The golden vales in his view.

All We Have
Andrew McFarland

When we were young punks, too young to get in,
We'd sneak in back doors to watch Hudson Falcons play.
At Benning all we had were the songs in our heads that we brought with us,
and the cadences we would chant as we marched.
On a remote mountain outpost, I sat on the hood of a MaxxPro, looking up at
the night sky. I chain smoked cigarettes and listened to every single Lucero
song.
When I got back, we drank all the whiskey we could get our hands on. We'd
scream Against Me! until our voices were gone.
In that moment nothing had changed, and we were still 17.
Years later, we wait for the bus, or on our way to school
We sing Disney songs or listen to T-Swift.
I'm older now
She helped calm me down, and gave me a new outlook.
Once the door is closed, it's my time. I put on Biggie and get ready to face
the day.

Full Circle
Matthew Sabedra

When I see you two, I see myself at that age
Innocently reenacting what I think war is like
But like in real life, my pretend wars were different
My kit was an old pistol belt and two wooden 1911s
But just like in your wars, the good guys always win
Today your kit is a plastic version of what I used in real war
When I see your faces as you ask how the real version of your toys work
My mind drifts to me asking the old vets the same thing
I feel a connection to them old men now
When I see the wonder in your eyes as I tell of foreign lands
When you two ask about the war, I must look how those old men did when I
asked the same thing many years ago
Like them, I church it up
The good guys win
We all come home
When you are older I will tell you two the truth

Forthcoming Books

Lucky Joe
- Leo Jenkins, Brian Kimber, David Rose

Addvice
- Keith Dow

About the Publisher

Dead Reckoning Collective is a veteran owned and operated publishing company. Our mission encourages literacy as a component of a positive lifestyle. Although DRC only publishes the written work of military veterans, the intention of closing the divide between civilians and veterans is held in the highest regard. By sharing these stories it is our hope that we can help to clarify how veterans should be viewed by the public and how veterans should view themselves.

Visit us at

deadreckoningco.com

Facebook: @deadreckoningco
Instagram: @deadreckoningcollective
Twitter: @dr_collective

Made in the USA
Columbia, SC
24 November 2020